Soho Theatre Company,
Chantal Arts and Theatre
and Hilary Williams

in association with Assembly Theatre
and Marshall Cordell present

T0348082

The Riot Group
in

switchtriptych

by Adriano Shaplin

First performed in workshop at the Ohio Theatre, New York on
20–21 July 2005

World premiere at Assembly Theatre as part of the
2005 Edinburgh Festival Fringe on 7 August 2005

The London season opened at Soho Theatre + Writers' Centre on
6 September 2005

www.theriotgroup.com

'Any man or woman who is devoutly Christian and works for the American Corporation is caught in an unseen vice whose pressure may split their mind from their soul. For the center of Christianity is a mystery, a son of God, and the center of the corporation is a detestation of mystery, a worship of technology. Nothing is more intrinsically opposed to technology than the bleeding heart of Christ.'

– Norman Mailer
Armies of the Night, 1967

'When old guys walk around and whistle it never seems like they're whistling any particular song.

It's always sorta random notes.

In the twenties and thirties I bet my grandfather probably stumbled upon half a dozen Beatles songs.

Didn't think anything of them,

Didn't think they were that good.

Didn't feel like showin' 'em to anyone.'

– Matt Cook
Old World Craftsmanship, 1998

The Riot Group in

switchtriptych

by Adriano Shaplin

Characters (in order of appearance)

LUCILLE	Stephanie Viola
PHILIPPA	Sarah Sanford
TRUMAN	Paul Schnabel
ANDREW	Drew Friedman
JUNE	Cassandra Friend

directed by	Adriano Shaplin
designed by	Jim Findlay
lighting design	William Cusick
sound design	Iver Findlay
dramaturg	Nina Steiger
technical director	William Cusick
production managers	Paul Lim (Edinburgh) Nick Ferguson (London)
lighting (London)	Christoph Wagner
press representation	Fiona Duff at Assembly (0131 226 2842) Nancy Poole at Soho Theatre (020 7478 0142)
graphic design	Huw Jenkins at snowcreative (www.snowcreative.co.uk)
producer	Louise Chantal (07976 418232)

SWITCH TRIPTYCH was developed as part of the New York Stage and Screen season at Vassar July 2005. The company would like to thank J Holtham at Vassar and Erich Jungwith at the Ohio Theatre for their support.

The producer would like to thank: The Riot Group; Maria Shaplin; William Burdett-Coutts and Marshall Cordell; Hilary and Stuart Williams; Mark Godfrey, Nina Steiger and Nick Ferguson at Soho Theatre; Fiona Duff, Claudia Courtis, Paul Lim, Melanie Smith and Mark Burlace and all at Assembly Theatre; James Hogan and all at Oberon Books; Ben Hall and Sally Whitehill at Curtis Brown; Mark Christian Subias; James Seabright and Festival Highlights, and Sean Hinds.

THE COMPANY

THE RIOT GROUP

The Riot Group is **Adriano Shaplin, Stephanie Viola, Drew Friedman, Paul Schnabel**, and **Maria Shaplin**. Since 1997, the Riot Group has created a series of critically-acclaimed original productions including *Wreck the Airline Barrier*, *Victory at the Dirt Palace*, and *Pugilist Specialist*. Since bringing their first production to the Edinburgh Festival in 1998, the company have won three Fringe Firsts, two Herald Angels, and been twice nominated for The Stage Acting Awards for Best Ensemble. Riot Group productions have played Off-West End, Off-Broadway, San Francisco, Glasgow, the Edinburgh Fringe, and most recently the Theater Der Welt Festival in Stuttgart Germany. All scripts are written by Adriano Shaplin with roles tailored for the ensemble. For more information about the company, including a complete archive of cuttings and production information, visit
www.theriotgroup.com

The **Switch Triptych** company also includes:

CASSANDRA FRIEND

Cassandra Friend has worked in the United Kingdom with companies including Theatre O, Sphinx, Hoipolloil and Angels in the Architecture. She has worked extensively in the United States and toured internationally with Pig Iron Theater Company. Productions included *Gentlemen Volunteers*, *Shut Eye* and *The Lucia Joyce Cabaret*. She is a graduate of Ecole Jacques Lecoq.

SARAH SANFORD

Sarah Sanford is a company member of Pig Iron Theater Company of Philadelphia. She first worked with Adriano Shaplin on Pig Iron's OBIE award-winning *Hell Meets Henry Halfway*, which played at the Ohio Theater in November 2004. Other Pig Iron productions include *Shut Eye*, *The Lucia Joyce Cabaret*, and *Measure for Measure*. Sarah studied theater at Swarthmore College and is a graduate of Ecole Jacques Lecoq.

PRODUCING PARTNERS

CHANTAL ARTS + THEATRE LTD

CAT was established in 2003 by Louise Chantal, who's previous production and marketing experience includes the Soho Theatre + Writers' Centre, Pleasance Theatres and Actors Touring Company. CAT specializes in working with new writing and international companies. 2004 productions include, with Soho Theatre Company, the Pulitzer Prize nominated, Fringe First and Herald Angel winning *Thom Pain (based on nothing)* by Will Eno with James Urbaniak (winner *The Stage* Best Actor Award, Edinburgh Festival) and Singularity's *How To Act Around Cops* (Fringe First winner.

Other productions include: The Riot Group's *Pugilist Specialist* (UK and US seasons and the Theater of the World Festival, Stuttgart 2005) and *Victory at the Dirt Palace* (UK tour); *Roadmovie* by Nick Whitfield and Wes Williams (Edinburgh Festival 2002 and UK/Eire Tour 2003); and *Silent Engine* by Julian Garner (with Pentabus Theatre – Fringe First winner 2002).

Louise Chantal joined Assembly Theatre as Theatre Producer in January 2005 and produces The Riot Group worldwide.

www.chantalarts.co.uk

ASSEMBLY THEATRE and MARSHALL CORDELL

2005 sees Assembly Theatre celebrate 25 years as 'the jewel in the crown of the fringe' (The Scotsman). Over that time Assembly has presented over 1500 productions including some of the world's most famous comedians, theatre companies and musicians. This year Assembly has joined forces with US producer Marshall Cordell to produce a wide-range of international theatre and comedians including The Riot Group.

www.assemblyrooms.com

HILARY WILLIAMS

has produced various West End shows, the latest being *The Postman Always Rings Twice* with Val Kilmer and Charlotte Emerson. She is a partner of Jorg Betts Associates and patron of Young Emerging Artists.

● soho
● theatre company

Soho Theatre Company is passionate in its commitment to new writing, producing a year-round programme of bold, original and accessible new plays – many of them from first-time playwrights.

'a foundry for new talent...one of the country's leading producers of new writing' Evening Standard

Soho Theatre + Writers' Centre offers an invaluable resource to emerging playwrights. Our training and outreach programme includes the innovative Under 11s scheme, the Young Writers' Group (15-25s) and a burgeoning series of Nuts and Bolts writing workshops designed to equip new writers with the basic tools of playwriting. We offer the nation's only unsolicited script-reading service, reporting on over 2,000 plays per year. We aim to develop and showcase the most promising new work through the national Verity Bargate Award, the Launch Pad scheme and the Writers' Attachment Programme, working to develop writers not just in theatre but also for TV and film.

'a creative hotbed...not only the making of theatre but the cradle for new screenplay and television scripts' The Times

Contemporary, comfortable, air-conditioned and accessible, Soho Theatre is busy from early morning to late at night. Alongside the production of new plays, it is also an intimate venue to see leading national and international comedians in an eclectic programme mixing emerging new talent with established names.

'London's coolest theatre by a mile' Midweek

● **soho**
● theatre company

Soho Theatre + Writers' Centre, 21 Dean St, London W1D 3NE

Admin: 020 7287 5060 ● Box Office: 0870 429 6883 ● Minicom: 020 7478 0136 ● www.sohotheatre.com ● email: box@sohotheatre.com

As well as being our neighbour just across Dean Street, TEQUILA\ is a leading sponsor of Soho Theatre. Because of their inviting reception area and alcoholic name, many passers-by think TEQUILA\ is a trendy bar. The truth is TEQUILA\ is a marketing agency with a difference. They make creativity part and parcel of everything they do. They have a unique working style called DISRUPTION, which helps clients take big steps forward in their business.

If you want to know more about them, visit **www.tequila-uk.com** or call Jenna Laxton on 020 7440 1130.

switchtriptych

First published in 2005 by Oberon Books Ltd
521 Caledonian Road, London N7 9RH
Tel: 020 7607 3637 / Fax: 020 7607 3629
e-mail: oberonbooks@btconnect.com
www.oberonbooks.com

A catalogue record for this book is available from the British
Library.

ISBN: 1 84002 621 9

Cover artwork by Huw Jenkins at snowcreative

Cover photograph by The Riot Group

Characters

LUCILLE

PHILIPPA

TRUMAN

ANDREW

JUNE

Voices of Irish Women

This play is dedicated to three women who have never met each other: Lucille Guzzino Viola, Philippa Dunham Shaplin, and Kristina Maria Ottolina Hagström. Thank you. – A. Shaplin

Act One

When the audience enters a red curtain hides the stage.

A mobile phone rings in the audience. It is a popular song. Recognizable.

The ring stops.

A message beep is heard.

Silence.

A generic mobile phone ring is heard. It rings then stops.

Silence.

A cordless phone rings. It stops.

A rotary phone rings. Stops.

We are travelling back in time.

The rings get older until we hear the crank and ring of a telephone box circa 1919.

Curtain opens slowly on this ring.

We see a telephone switchboard exchange, New York City, 1919.

There are three large switchboards running the length of the stage. Maybe there are two obscured switchboards on either side, disappearing into the wings. The center switchboard is dead center. Seated on a stool in front of the center switchboard is LUCILLE, a switchboard operator in her late twenties. She is facing the audience. Stage right, seated with her back to the audience is PHILIPPA, a switchboard operator in her twenties. She is attending to her board. The stage-left board is vacant, an empty stool in front of it. Upstage, behind the boards is an area roughly defined as the management office. TRUMAN, an office manager in his middle fifties, wanders a bit, looking at nothing, drinking coffee and reading the newspaper.

Upstage right JUNE, a prospective operator, stands with her arms out-stretched, facing away from the audience. ANDREW, an office manager in his early thirties, is using a paper tape-measure to calculate her height, reach, waist-size, the distance between her hands and elbows, feet and knees. He is going slowly and recording the measurements on a scrap of paper. Far upstage center there is an upright piano. TRUMAN and ANDREW occasionally play it.

LUCILLE is a very tiny young Italian-American woman dressed entirely in black. A veil covers her eyes and nose as if she is in mourning. There is a full glass in her hand and an open bottle of champagne on the floor next to her. She is smirking and stares directly at the audience. She is drunk and remains so throughout the play. She is steady and motionless, and becomes more articulate the more she drinks. She is absolutely positive that she is the protagonist, suspects she might also be the narrator and this is reflected through her behavior.

LUCILLE and PHILIPPA wear headsets with mouthpieces, but LUCILLE's is hanging around her neck.

It is raining very hard outside and we hear it. A bucket catches drops from the ceiling.

We also hear the sounds of a telephone exchange, as if our characters are in a room with twenty other operators, unseen. Occasional pops, twerps, cranks, and 'old-fashioned' voices buzz underneath the dialogue.

Whenever an operator speaks on her line, the customer's voice should bleed through. That the actors are interacting with recordings and loops doesn't need to be disguised.

PHILIPPA stealthily unwraps a sucking candy but the noise is conspicuous. She pops the candy in her mouth. It is 6:15 in the morning.

Throughout the play there is a stillness that makes any physical gesture or pause pregnant with meaning. Whenever action is suggested in stage directions, it should be prominent.

LUCILLE: I take a carriage to Hell's Kitchen just to scald my tongue.

Pause.

Guido in un trasporto a Hell's Kitchen per bruciare la mia lingua.
Only at night when the lines are short.

PHILIPPA: (*Into her mouthpiece.*) Good morning Mr Fillmore...

LUCILLE: They've got cauldrons screaming with flavor and smoke.
And prize-fighters pull out my chairs.
That's because they know who I am.

ANDREW: (*To JUNE.*) Keep your arms up.

JUNE sighs and raises her arms slightly.

PHILIPPA: Mr Fillmore I'm sorry to interrupt, but this isn't Agatha.

Pause.

This isn't Agatha.

Pause.

I'm not Agatha.

Pause.

Married I'm afraid.

LUCILLE takes a big gulp from her glass.

LUCILLE: Big-boned girls blow me kisses in the Bowery.
Top-hats send over beers with corks whom I ignore, the men.
Snake-charmers beg for nickels in Soho. That's right.
Near-beer pikers steer clear in Noho. They do.
That's because they know who I am.
And they say:
Quando finisce la partita, i pedoni, le torri, i cavalli, i vescovi, i due re e le due regine tutti vanno nello stesso scatolo.
I don't think so. No.

TRUMAN: (*To ANDREW.*) Did you see this?

ANDREW: Working.

TRUMAN: You can't listen?

ANDREW: No. (*To JUNE.*) Arms up.

JUNE: They were. They are.

ANDREW: Now.

LUCILLE: Chinamen keep my secrets.
Krauts leave sausages wrapped in butcher paper at my feet.
My driver is pleased to wait. Never let them see you walk.

JUNE: Will I be wearing a uniform?

ANDREW: Not really.

PHILIPPA: Good morning Mr Carnegie? Excuse me, Mrs Carnegie.

Pause.

I will hold.

LUCILLE: This is how it started.

She drinks.

First God made light, 'cause He couldn't see what the hell He
was making.
And the monkeys were His pets.
And on the second day He made mankind and womankind.
Depending on your denomination.
And He made the snake for temptation.
And the snake said 'eat it'.
And He took out his rib to hit the snake,
'Cause that's the villain.
And then He made the Empire State Building.
And nothing good ever happened again.

She drinks.

PHILIPPA: I like the last part there yeah about the snake.

LUCILLE: Dio era nato in Italia.
Good girls go to heaven. I Santi vanno Italia.
Italy is heaven on a long weekend.
Just the same. I'm never going back.

PHILIPPA: You'll go back. Mr Carnegie?

LUCILLE drinks.

TRUMAN: Unbelievable.

ANDREW: What? What is it? I'm measuring the new girl. I have
to measure the new girl. Okay? Can I measure the new girl?
Can I do this?

Pause.

What is it?

TRUMAN: Nothing.

ANDREW: No. I'm stopped. (*He folds up his measuring tape.*) I
stopped. See? So let us hear it.

TRUMAN: It's nothing.

ANDREW: It is now. Now it is.

Pause.

TRUMAN: I lost a bit of money on a horse.

Pause.

PHILIPPA unwraps a sucking candy.

ANDREW: I hope you're happy. (*He unwinds his measuring tape.*)

LUCILLE: Stray cats follow me to work.
They wait below my window.
Multiplying.
Planning to take over Brooklyn.
I'm providing simultaneous translation. We'll see how that goes.

I'm a proud traitor to the human race. Or at least to Brooklyn. Brooklyn. Schiuma fango.

She drinks.

PHILIPPA: You've never been to Brooklyn.

LUCILLE: Even a peasant has dignity in Gotham. You never show they're toes in public.

PHILIPPA looks at her feet. Her shoes are off.

PHILIPPA: What? My feet are killing me Lu.

LUCILLE: It is our distaste for feet that separate us from the animal kingdom Pippa, are you lemur? Are you a tree monkey?

PHILIPPA: Anyway I've got stockings on.

LUCILLE: Or are you a modern woman circa the year nineteen hundred and nineteen?

PHILIPPA: What's a lemur?

LUCILLE: What is it?

PHILIPPA: Yeah.

Pause.

LUCILLE: It is a type of gorilla. A Forbearance.

PHILIPPA: Huh. Yeah.

Pause.

Are you making that up?

LUCILLE: Shh.

JUNE: (*Arms still outstretched.*) What's my wingspan?

ANDREW: What?

JUNE: My wingspan?

ANDREW: You aren't being paid for training so you might
wanna can it with the riddles and let me do my ever-lovin' job.

JUNE: Oh sorry.

ANDREW: It's English Only on the boards, you should know
that. Did they tell you that? You should get used to speaking
English.

JUNE: I'll do my best.

TRUMAN: (*To PHILIPPA.*) Pippa?

*At this point TRUMAN has put down the paper and is reading a
large, leather-bound book. PHILIPPA holds up a hand to stop him
speaking.*

PHILIPPA: This isn't Agatha.

Pause.

I'm not Agatha.

TRUMAN: Sorry. It can wait.

PHILIPPA: Ha? Just wait.

*LUCILLE's board starts ringing. TRUMAN stares at her.
LUCILLE is still, staring out. She drinks. She doesn't answer the
call.*

JUNE: What happens with this?

ANDREW: Excuse me.

JUNE: These measurements.

Pause.

I hope you can keep a secret.

ANDREW: (*Not understanding the joke.*) What?

JUNE: What happens with these?

ANDREW: Whadda you think?

JUNE: I really have no idea.

ANDREW: If you can't reach you'll be slow.

JUNE: Why are you measuring my waist?

ANDREW: It's not fun for me either.

JUNE: Some might call it indelicate.

ANDREW: What are you implying?

JUNE: I'm not implying.

ANDREW: What?

JUNE: Why are you measuring my waist?

ANDREW: Truman?

TRUMAN: (*Looking up from his book.*) Yes?

ANDREW: Why do we measure the waist?

TRUMAN: Ahhhh. Hm. Is it to see if they're pregnant?

ANDREW: (*To JUNE.*) To see if you're pregnant?

JUNE: I don't know.

ANDREW: You asked.

TRUMAN: Is it to see if they've had children?

ANDREW: Anyway, are you pregnant?

JUNE: NO.

ANDREW: Then you've got nothing to worry about.

TRUMAN: I honestly don't know.

ANDREW: Yeah thanks.

JUNE: I want a copy of all those figures.

ANDREW: You can't ask for that. You can't demand that. You can't demand that of me. That's a demand the way you phrased it in case you noticed.

JUNE: You will copy those figures out for me.

ANDREW: You aren't being paid for training.

PHILIPPA: Bob? It's 6:30. Yes. Time to wake up. Yes. Sorry about that. You won't be late. It's fifteen minutes! I was doing Agatha's calls. Yesterday. Mm-hm. Okay sweetie. Okay honey. Don't fall back asleep. I will not call you back. I'm afraid I'm busy tonight. Yes. Yes. Good morning.

LUCILLE: Boy did we clobber the trains. Annuncio. Think about it.

TRUMAN: (*Out loud, absentmindedly.*) Anyway it's the sociologists that ask for the data. It doesn't have anything to do with us.

ANDREW: We're past it Truman thanks.

TRUMAN: Huh? Tell her we're just working stiffs like her.

ANDREW: Weeellll. Not quite. (*To JUNE.*) Not quite.

TRUMAN: Tell her we're just one step higher on the food chain than she is and that it's our job to dispassionately implement the technologies and managerial directives –

ANDREW: Thanks Truman. I think she heard you. That's great.

Something like a mechanical roar is heard off-stage. TRUMAN snaps his fingers at ANDREW and they both exit into the wings.

LUCILLE: Tell me who'll take a train?
Get Dows Dunham on the horn.
I'll apologize personally the damage we done his industry.
Who'll take a train when all you need is a call-box and this widow to reach out and touch somebody?
Mark that it's mine.
Toilet with wheels you ask me. Trains.

And what place is worth dragging your body apart from lovely
New York City?
Forget mother back in Kansas,
She'll have to settle for a phone call.
Thirty minutes every Sunday saves you a backache and train fare.
Not to mention the fortune you save on pencils and stationery.
God forgive us we clobbered correspondence. And nobody
misses it!
Death to the love-note. Good riddance.
How many stately redwoods died for the cause of some
amateur Lothario?
Scribbling his banal longing so a dizzy half-wit can 'treasure' it
forever?
Charm her grandkids to tears reciting granddad's quaint
rambling:
'Missing you like the desert misses the rain.'
Mark that, it's mine.
No, it's all phone calls now.
Pony up and whisper your sweet nothings on the wire
Sono secreti protegganno per nostra silenzia.

PHILIPPA: Jeffrey sent a letter.

LUCILLE drinks.

LUCILLE: You are forgiven your nostalgia Pippa, I know your
heart's in the right place.

PHILIPPA: What does it mean when they cut parts out?

LUCILLE: Babbling about troop movement no doubt. Not the
brightest pebble. I'm giving him points though, you know, for
presuming you'd be interested.

PHILIPPA: But I'm not.

LUCILLE: Not his fault.

PHILIPPA: We only had one dance. I hope I'm not the only gal
he writes to.

LUCILLE: Then again a spiteful censor might razor out the odd dirty word, rob you your cheap thrills. Perhaps he waxed about his neglected body in medical detail hoping you'd have yourself a one-handed read.

PHILIPPA: Lucille!

LUCILLE sets her glass down carefully then pounds her chair once in frustration. TRUMAN and ANDREW re-enter.

LUCILLE: Goddam censors. Al' inferno con loro! Can't a girl enjoy a few filthy lines about 'troop movement'? Hack out the dirty bits and we're left with nothing but anecdotes about the food.

PHILIPPA: Always about the food! Jeepers. And how bad it is.

LUCILLE: Oh, Miss Cheese Sandwiches and Chocolate Milk over here. Not that he'd get much better at your cold-water flat. You could at least master a roast for crying out loud Pippa what if I want to drop by? Con i panini formaggio, Christ.

PHILIPPA: I told ya to call before you drop by! (*Effortlessly, she lets it go.*) Anyway I hardly know him. Here – (*PHILIPPA holds the letter out to LUCILLE.*) – bless this that he loses my address or something.

LUCILLE: (*Whilst casually casting an Italian peasant curse over the letter.*) Be glad they don't put phones on the front lines.

PHILIPPA's board rings.

They'd never get any killing done and we'd suffer daily the details of sock rot.

PHILIPPA: Number please.

LUCILLE: Tell the Wright Brother's I said I'm sorry.
Who needs your plane?
Uncle Sam might use it to light up a city now and again
But no right-thinking Yankee with a telephone is going to risk life and limb just to see a place!

What's to see?
There's nothing left and less to come! Stay indoors. It's not
getting any better out there.
Keep your slippers on.

PHILIPPA: (*Into her mouthpiece.*) Thank you. (*To LUCILLE.*) I'd
like to take a flight. Go somewhere with swell food.

LUCILLE: WHAT? Oh dear God forget about the food. Do you
like tongue?

PHILIPPA: Tongue?

LUCILLE: Cow tongue. In other countries they eat tongue and
eye-balls. That's probably a sin. If you went digging, that's a sin.

PHILIPPA: I suppose if it's cooked properly. At least from a recipe.

LUCILLE: You'll be using your taste-buds to taste taste-buds. It
isn't Catholic.

PHILIPPA: I'm adventurous.

LUCILLE: I'm adventurous. Speaking of which, let's ring those
Mick chicks in Boston. I hate those rosy-cheeked pigs.

PHILIPPA: Oh yes, let's call them. They're funny.

LUCILLE: That's the devil in them, wriggling up out of their
mouths like a hairy red snake.

PHILIPPA: At least they're having a little bit of –

LUCILLE: Suuuurrrreeee, with they're little accents and Gaelic
curse words and jolly sisterhood. But let me tell you: Every
one of those paddy birds –

PHILIPPA: What's that song they taught us?

LUCILLE: Taught you. Oh you were intoxicated by them. You
think they're exotic because you're not from New York.

PHILIPPA: You're not from New York.

LUCILLE: Every last one of those paddy birds comes home to a beer bag of a husband and ten screaming piglets rushing for the tit. And when they aren't nursing they're conspiring to burn the house down. Irish children are maniacs.

PHILIPPA: That's the word. They sound 'jolly'.

LUCILLE: They all get knocked around. Sleep on the cold side of the bed.

PHILIPPA: So should I call them?

LUCILLE: Call them call them, remind me why I hate that pigsty Boston. Heh. 'The mean streets of Boston.' Freckled pigs.

PHILIPPA unwraps a sucking candy while dialing the number of the exchange station in Boston. LUCILLE finishes her glass and holds it out to PHILIPPA without looking at her. PHILIPPA stares at it, then picks the champagne bottle off the floor and pours.

JUNE: You're not very friendly.

ANDREW: I'm not your friend.

JUNE: Would you like to know what I did before this?

Pause.

I plied the needles that fashioned comforts for our soldiers and volunteered by fingers to be pricked and crusted over with these near pre-historic scales. See. (*She shows him her fingertips.*) Calluses this enormous respond to neither balm nor salve. These are permanent rough spots on my otherwise flawlessly smooth body.

On 'body' ANDREW snaps his paper measuring tape.

ANDREW: Shit.

PHILIPPA laughs loudly at something on her line. ANDREW thinks, momentarily that the laughter is directed at him.

PHILIPPA: No doll it's Pippa in New York.

JUNE: In exchange for my labor I received an unusually generous salary and temporary reprieve from the pressure to marry; a blessing to this girl, picky as I am; but ultimately unsatisfactory.

Pause.

Did you know there is a lone female coal miner in Bayonne Wisconsin? She successfully masqueraded as a man for six years until her filthy blouse was blown asunder in a minor accident. She was unharmed, but her sex revealed. They allowed her to stay on as she was a fierce worker and indispensable to the line.

PHILIPPA: Truman, I'm using the PA.

PHILIPPA patches her line into LUCILLE's head-set and the audience can now hear both sides of the conversation. The Boston exchange station sounds rammed with raucous Irish women, nearly screaming with laughter at their own jokes. The primary voice belongs to Ms Patricia Kenny. The second voice belongs to Ms Mally O'Murphy. The following unfolds like an old radio talk show, with the Irish women playing the parts of host, co-host, and audience. LUCILLE and PHILIPPA are the guests.

Hey everybody, it's Room Three at the Boston Exchange!

Ms Kenny: Miss Pippa, Miss Pippa. Lovely of you to drop by.

Ms O'Murphy: It's Pippa girls, say hello. Remember the pink skirt?

PHILIPPA: It was barely pink. Anyway, Lucille's here to the left of me.

Ms Kenny: Lucille, how's that old sour puss getting on?

Ms O'Murphy: She's saying how the hell are you Lucille?

Ms Kenny: How ya doing?

Ms O'Murphy: Still got a 'No Irish Need Apply' sign hanging on your bedroom door?

Ms Kenny: On the third post on her four poster bed is more like.

LUCILLE: And sewn into my knickers you barbarian. Tell me which of your children did you eat for dinner last night?

There is audible disapproval from the Irish operators.

Ms Kenny: Wellll, the youngest of course.

Screams of laughter in the background.

Ms O'Murphy: That's what you call veal scaloppini down in your Little Italy!

More screams.

LUCILLE: Well, that's one down, better get busy with your man making another.

There are 'oooooo's from the Irish operators.

Ms Kenny: I might just do that Ms Lucille.

LUCILLE: Soak your stockings in Guinness, he'll find his way to your bedroom.

Screams of laughter. Cat-calls.

Ms O'Murphy: How about you Pippa? How are you in that department?

PHILIPPA: (*Lazy, almost sing-songy.*) I'm fiiiinnnneeee.

Ms Kenny: When are you going to come to Boston and earn a living?

LUCILLE: She's not going to join your filthy union.

Ms Kenny: Paying those New York City prices without a shred of job security, you're smarter than that Pippa.

PHILIPPA: (*Lazy, sing-songy.*) I do okaaaaayyy.

The Irish women coo.

LUCILLE: Last I heard your stinking coven was Irish only paddy bird.

Ms Kenny: We can make an exception for any woman what loves the pope; even you you sour wop dwarf.

The Irish women cheer.

LUCILLE: Don't evoke the pope to me you paddy-come-lately, my pope doesn't love a red-haired monkey pagan pretending at Roman dignity. Scramble for your boxing gloves Mick, I hear your man wants to 'snuggle'.

Ms Kenny: Good morning to you Pippa, the mayor of Boston sends his regards.

Ms O'Murphy: Let's hear it for Miss Pippa girls, let's hear it.

There is applause heard on the line. The call is terminated. LUCILLE has finished her champagne and now pulls a bottle of whiskey from beneath her switchboard.

LUCILLE: That was awful. (*Gesturing with the whiskey bottle.*) Who's for coffee?

PHILIPPA: I wish I was Irish.

LUCILLE: Treacherous waters those: Envy. Coffee?

PHILIPPA: Sure.

LUCILLE: Get the cups and the coffee.

PHILIPPA: What am I, English? That's no fun.

PHILIPPA's board rings. She moves to answer it.

LUCILLE: You aren't English Pippa, forget England. That was always the point. Get us coffee.

PHILIPPA: Number please?

LUCILLE: Christ.

ANDREW: Alright, we're done.

JUNE: Is that it then?

ANDREW: Yes, that's it. Just run on home and collect your paychecks. Payday is Friday.

Pause.

NO! That isn't it! You haven't even been trained!

JUNE: I glanced at the manual.

ANDREW: You haven't even been trained. Did you say glanced? You didn't say glanced. Because the manual should be memorized. You were supposed to fucking memorize it for today.

On 'fucking' PHILIPPA gasps. TRUMAN says, 'Hey!'

PHILIPPA: Swell language Ethel! I could hear that through the cans.

TRUMAN: We don't need that Andrew. You could hear that through the cans?

PHILIPPA: Oh pos-i-lute-ly! (*Into her mouthpiece.*) You here that Gert? She heard it.

TRUMAN: She heard that through the cans.

ANDREW: Allow me to introduce you to... (*Gesturing toward TRUMAN.*)

TRUMAN: No. Is it time? I'm not ready.

ANDREW: I thought – ?

ANDREW grabs his manual. TRUMAN grabs his manual.

TRUMAN: What page?

ANDREW: Are you at the chapter on training?

TRUMAN: Yes thank you.

ANDREW: Page twenty-two. Your turn!

JUNE: What you don't have it memorized?

ANDREW: That's it, I'm through with this quiff. (*ANDREW ditches his manual.*) This is Truman, he is your supervisor.

PHILIPPA: Hey Mac, what if one of my callers heard that noise? The complaint's gonna stick to me.

ANDREW: I thought one of your callers did hear it?

PHILIPPA: Sure but that was just Gert. I'm saying if I'm talking to a square of something.

ANDREW: You mean a customer? You let me know if that happens.

PHILIPPA: Oh now he's snapping his cap at me.

ANDREW: Kill it Pippa.

PHILIPPA: Yeah, I'll 'kill it' Ethel.

TRUMAN: Andrew, can I talk to you?

ANDREW: What? And she's (*Indicating JUNE.*) a difficult one. I'm not above reporting it. First day or none.

TRUMAN: (*To JUNE.*) Excuse us, I'll be with you in a second.

ANDREW: Why are they bringing new girls in anyway? Aren't we –

TRUMAN: Shhh. I need a sponsor.

Pause.

ANDREW looks at the book in TRUMAN's hands.

ANDREW: What the hell are you reading?

TRUMAN: It's a book.

ANDREW grabs the book, gestures with it momentarily, then tosses it across the stage.

ANDREW: Oh goddam Salvation-Army-soup-kitchen-holier-than-thou-s. What convinced them the whole world needs improving?

TRUMAN: It isn't the Salvation Army. It's a club for…

Pause.

My wife wants me to stop drinking.

ANDREW: Ann?

TRUMAN: That's my wife.

ANDREW: A teetotaler?

TRUMAN: Her?

ANDREW: Are they Mormons?

TRUMAN: No.

ANDREW moves to retrieve the book.

ANDREW: Quakers?

TRUMAN: It isn't religious.

ANDREW: Jewish?

TRUMAN: It's non-religious.

ANDREW: Atheists?

TRUMAN: Not anti-religious. I don't remember the word.

JUNE: Nondenominational.

ANDREW: (*Turning to JUNE, annoyed.*) I'm not beneath reporting you. I swear to God. Most girls don't train during the early shift.

JUNE: Why? Because it's so busy?

Pause.

LUCILLE is taking a quick slug from her whiskey bottle.

Pause.

PHILIPPA giggles. LUCILLE sees that PHILIPPA is disengaged and raises the whiskey bottle again to indicate she wants coffee. PHILIPPA misses it. At this point the audience might wonder if LUCILLE is disabled. She is not.

JUNE: They told me to come at six.

On the word 'come' ANDREW turns back to TRUMAN.

ANDREW: Have you ever met a teetotaler? Wait: Is your wife a teetotaler?

TRUMAN: No. I said.

ANDREW: Have you ever met a teetotaler?

TRUMAN: I'll ask someone else.

ANDREW: Find one. Look her in the eyes.

PHILIPPA: Lu, your bookie's on five.

LUCILLE: Ace!

LUCILLE spins around and uses her board for the first time.

TRUMAN: I'll ask someone else.

LUCILLE: What's the score?

ANDREW: Something missing there.

TRUMAN: Well Ann wants me to drink less.

ANDREW: Less or never?

Pause. They stare at each other.

TRUMAN: I'll ask someone else.

ANDREW: A wise man said –

TRUMAN grabs the book out of ANDREW's hands.

LUCILLE: Ethel doesn't know any wise men.

ANDREW: A wise man said – thank you Lucille – a wise man said –

LUCILLE: (*Still on the phone with her bookie.*) No I'm here.

TRUMAN: Forget I asked.

ANDREW: 'Sobriety, properly executed, makes one mean and avuncular.'

JUNE: 'Avuncular' means 'friendly'.

Pause.

LUCILLE pulls her headphones off.

ANDREW: Well that's not the way it sounds.

LUCILLE: Who's speaking please?

PHILIPPA: New girl.

LUCILLE: Are you done? Coffee please.

PHILIPPA's board rings.

Shit.

ANDREW: (*To himself.*) Shit. 'Sobriety, properly executed, makes one…'

TRUMAN: Lay off already.

ANDREW: At best, you're too old to change Son.

TRUMAN: Says you. What's 'son'?

ANDREW: Come to think of it. Yes. I'll do it.

TRUMAN: You could be my son. Do what?

ANDREW: I'll sponsor you Sonny. Don't say I never did anything for you.

Pause.

TRUMAN: What's the catch?

JUNE: Excuse me.

ANDREW: I'll be watching you.

ANDREW grabs the book out of TRUMAN's hands.

Train the new girl.

TRUMAN: I'm –

ANDREW: You've got to focus on work.

LUCILLE: (*Hangs up her phone.*) Ha! (*Pours whiskey into her glass.*) I
might get emotional. There's no telling.

*TRUMAN and JUNE are staring at each other. ANDREW
appears stage right of PHILIPPA with a tray of mugs and a coffee
pot. PHILIPPA holds up two fingers while continuing on her line.
ANDREW doesn't pour.*

TRUMAN: You're?

JUNE: June.

TRUMAN: What's that?

JUNE: Hm?

TRUMAN: Are you Irish?

JUNE: I'm English.

TRUMAN: Hm. What are the English good at?

JUNE: Well you won't catch me complaining about the rain.

TRUMAN: (*Pause.*) I mean your trade.

JUNE: Previously I plied the needles that fashioned comforts for
our soldiers.

TRUMAN: What happened?

Pause.

JUNE: We won.

TRUMAN: Oh. That.

PHILIPPA: Pour!

ANDREW: 'Please'?

PHILIPPA: Pour you lousy Bohunk. Bank's closed.

ANDREW: Check.

PHILIPPA: Oh yeah I doubt it

> *ANDREW pours the coffee. TRUMAN has brought JUNE to the threshold between switchboards.*

TRUMAN: So let's.

JUNE: Mm?

TRUMAN: So let's us sit down then, and get started.

PHILIPPA: (*Handing a mug to LUCILLE.*) I think Ethel's stuck on me.

ANDREW: Yeah.

LUCILLE: You could do worse.

> *LUCILLE dumps the contents of her whiskey glass into the coffee.*

JUNE: (*Looking at the girls.*) Hello.

PHILIPPA: (*To LUCILLE.*) You're in the pocket today.

LUCILLE: Got a lead on a bet.

PHILIPPA: Heavy sugar?

LUCILLE: Heh?

PHILIPPA: Good money?

LUCILLE: What, you bet?

PHILIPPA: Nah.

JUNE: My name is June.

LUCILLE and PHILIPPA do not respond.

LUCILLE: You should come in on this one.

PHILIPPA: Horses?

LUCILLE: Negroes. Our man's Kimbo Slice, just out of Riker's.

PHILIPPA: Fighting?

LUCILLE: Mac says he's undefeated in the Riker's yard. We're betting on his eye-popping left hook.

PHILIPPA: Oh that's disgusting.

PHILIPPA's board rings and she answers it

TRUMAN: Why don't you take a seat?

JUNE: Friendly bunch.

PHILIPPA: That's your other man.

LUCILLE: Patch it through!

PHILIPPA: I think it's Ralph.

LUCILLE: (*Speaking into her head-set.*) Who's that Ralph? Hey Charlie. That's right. I should think so. As I expected. Whadda ya want me to do about it.

Screaming is heard from the mouthpiece. LUCILLE moves the receiver away from her ear.

'Cause that's – 'cause that's – hey pipe down you son of bitch! – 'cause two hundred doesn't buy a month any more asshole – it gets you two weeks at the top of my list, and any list of any girl underneath me. Yes, including your second line. (*She shakes her head 'no'.*) Everybody else is paying one-twenty-five a week. Yes one-twenty-five. Milt is paying that.

Pause.

Because I used to like ya, but I don't anymore. That's why. I'll put you down for two-hundred for two weeks – and that's how you'll pay me, twice a month – that's a hundred less than I'm charging Milt take it or leave it. Always a pleasure.

She hangs up.

PHILIPPA: That Charlie?

LUCILLE: Ha?

PHILIPPA: I said was that Charlie.

LUCILLE: I'm keeping track Pippa.

PHILIPPA: I know.

LUCILLE: Do you?

ANDREW: Pippa, can you – ?

PHILIPPA: Write it down then.

LUCILLE: You write down you're so worried. I remember it.

PHILIPPA: Just so we agree it was Charlie.

LUCILLE: Pippa.

PHILIPPA: And we agree that I fielded it.

LUCILLE: You'll get your cut!

PHILIPPA: Okay jeez don't blow a gasket for crying out loud.

LUCILLE: Greedy!

PHILIPPA: Oh lay off will ya?

LUCILLE: Mmm. (*LUCILLE makes a kiss face and noise.*) I love ya kid.

ANDREW: Client?

LUCILLE: You know who it was and what it was about bone-jangles, leave me in peace.

ANDREW: Don't we pay you enough Philippa?

PHILIPPA: Just a client Ethel, checking to make sure his business phone is listed correctly.

ANDREW: They're a nervous sort. Those business owners. Always calling around checking to see if their business phone is listed correctly.

LUCILLE: They wouldn't have a pot to piss in wasn't for Bell Atlantic. Cheers. Salute.

ANDREW: Pot to piss in? That's lovely.

LUCILLE: (*She notices ANDREW.*) You are the biggest Jew I've ever seen. You should be the king of Jews.

ANDREW: I'm half-Jewish.

LUCILLE: What's the other half? Skyscraper?

PHILIPPA: Oh funny yeah.

LUCILLE: He's the spawn of David and Goliath. Who knew? It wasn't a fight. It was a custody battle.

ANDREW: A custody battle?

LUCILLE: I said it. Solomon and what not.

PHILIPPA: It's good Andrew. Tall is good.

ANDREW: Pippa?

PHILIPPA: Andrew.

ANDREW: What?

PHILIPPA: You 'what'? (*Philippa's board rings then, with false courtesy.*) Can you excuse me for a second Andrew?

ANDREW: (*Pauses. Looks down.*) I forgot what I needed from you.

PHILIPPA: Jake. (*PHILIPPA swings back around.*)

ANDREW: Damnit.

LUCILLE: Here's to you Ethel.

TRUMAN: Okay, let's begin.

JUNE: Alright.

Pause.

TRUMAN is seated on the other side of June's board and must duck his head around to talk to her.

TRUMAN: Okay, let's assume the line lights up.

Pause.

I'm not going to turn the board on.

JUNE: What?

TRUMAN: This is just for practice.

JUNE: I know.

TRUMAN: So?

JUNE: What?

TRUMAN: Pretend it's ringing.

JUNE: I am.

TRUMAN: So then you answer.

JUNE: Oh! 'Number please.'

TRUMAN: Okay, let's hold on for a moment.

JUNE: Okay.

TRUMAN: With a little more courtesy please.

JUNE: Courtesy. Alright.

Pause.

TRUMAN: Listen do you need me to make a ringing noise?

JUNE: Maybe.

TRUMAN: Alright so I'll make a ringing noise and that will be your cue.

LUCILLE: Hang on a minute, Pippa get off your line.

PHILIPPA: (*To a customer.*) Excuse me Mr Johns I think you did something wrong.

She yanks a cord out to end his call.

What's doing?

LUCILLE: Andrew!

ANDREW: What?

TRUMAN: Excuse me Lu but I'm trying to –

LUCILLE: Boss is going to do a ringing noise. Carry on Truman.

Pause.

All attention is now on TRUMAN, who looks stricken and then moves out of sight. Pause.

TRUMAN: 'Ring.'

PHILIPPA and ANDREW applaud. LUCILLE smiles, then sets her glass down carefully to join the applause.

LUCILLE: Beautiful. Pip, what happened to Agatha?

PHILIPPA: Did you just notice that she was gone?

LUCILLE: She ain't gone doll, might have shrunk some three inches.

PHILIPPA: (*Whispering.*) That's Agatha's replacement.

LUCILLE: (*Now whispering.*) Huh? Why is she ignoring us?

PHILIPPA: First day.

LUCILLE: Stuck up tart.

JUNE: I said 'hello'!

ANDREW: (*To TRUMAN.*) Thirsty? How you doing?

TRUMAN: Busy.

ANDREW: Had a drink yet?

TRUMAN: No.

ANDREW: How long's it been?

TRUMAN: Four hours.

ANDREW: Good. Only about fifty-thousand to go.

TRUMAN: Fifty-thousand? To go until what?

ANDREW: I was guessing.

TRUMAN: That's only five years! Until what? Until I'm dead? You think I'll be dead in five years?

ANDREW: Fine. One hundred thousand hours.

TRUMAN: Ten years? Dead? In ten years?

ANDREW: Sure. And that's if you quit drinking.

TRUMAN: Don't you think quitting would likely extend my life?

ANDREW: Well I shouldn't think so.

TRUMAN: You could die tomorrow. You don't know how things are going to turn out.

ANDREW: Alright.

TRUMAN: It's a crap-shoot. You could die next week.

ANDREW: Okay.

TRUMAN: I could live to be eighty.

ANDREW: Eighty?!

TRUMAN: Maybe!

Pause.

ANDREW disengages.

Pause.

I'm going to have to do the ring again aren't I?

JUNE: Jesus I'm sorry. 'Number please.'

TRUMAN: Alright, let's hold on.

LUCILLE: Did you hear that?

PHILIPPA: What?

LUCILLE: That wasn't proper American English.

PHILIPPA: She's a yank. Or…what am I trying to say?

LUCILLE: Yank's what they call us. Is this a put on?

TRUMAN: Lu.

LUCILLE: Is this a put on?

PHILIPPA: So what am I trying to say?

LUCILLE: Red coat. She's putting us on.

PHILIPPA: No foolin? Is this a put on?

LUCILLE: What I'm askin'.

TRUMAN: Lu?

LUCILLE: This is me! Is this a put on?

Pause.

JUNE: No. I'm English.

Pause.

It's not a put on.

LUCILLE: Come on, spill the beans.

PHILIPPA: Is it a put on?

JUNE: No, I'm. (*She faces out.*) I'm not American.

PHILIPPA: No foolin'?

LUCILLE: 'Cause if this is a put on I'm put off.

JUNE: You're put off?

LUCILLE points her finger directly at JUNE.

TRUMAN: Lu?

LUCILLE: Woooo talk back.

TRUMAN: Lu, lay off will you I gotta train the –

PHILIPPA: You from Britain or just England?

JUNE: England.

LUCILLE: The Kingdom of England.

PHILIPPA: Do you know John Philips?

JUNE: No.

PHILIPPA: Well he's from England.

JUNE: Yes.

TRUMAN: Lu?

PHILIPPA: What, am I a sap for asking?

JUNE: No!

LUCILLE: Oh she's got her nose in the air. Think that accent makes you clever?

JUNE: I don't.

LUCILLE: You sure? How about more clever than me? More clever than me?

TRUMAN gets up and walks away.

JUNE: Come on.

LUCILLE: Do you have any proof that you're cleverer than me? Or your kind? Do you and your merry kind have any proof to prop your nose in the air? Any proof? I know you've got your noses in the air. Got any proof for that? Anything like jazz or movies or tall buildings or tycoons or maybe the odd vegetable?

JUNE: I don't think I'm cleverer than anyone.

LUCILLE: You don't think you just know.

JUNE: If you're talking about England...

LUCILLE: I think I am. Amn't I? Duchess Pippa? Amn't I talking about merry old England?

PHILIPPA: Ignore her, she's bent.

JUNE: If you're talking about England, than I think my country is distinguished by the absence of things like tycoons and tall buildings. Not to mention slavery. As long as we're comparing.

Pause.

TRUMAN notices ANDREW sipping from a cup.

TRUMAN: What are you doing?

LUCILLE: Well she came prepared didn't she Pip?

PHILIPPA: With what?

ANDREW: What?

TRUMAN: What are you drinking?

LUCILLE: She's got a whole thing to say I think.

ANDREW: Irish coffee.

PHILIPPA: Oh.

TRUMAN: Well what's that about?

ANDREW: I've had my breakfast.

TRUMAN: But you're my sponsor.

ANDREW: Well I'm not giving you any.

Pause.

What – I'm not allowed to drink? Give me that book.

ANDREW finishes his drink as TRUMAN fetches the book.

Forget the book. That doesn't make any sense. I'm not trying to quit drinking.

TRUMAN: Well it's no good tempting me.

ANDREW: Well that's just one of the bridges we'll need to cross together. Temptation will be your biggest challenge.

TRUMAN: I know that.

ANDREW: So? (*He sips from the cup.*) You're welcome.

Pause.

You finish with the new girl?

LUCILLE: (*To JUNE.*) You look uncomfortable.

JUNE: I am, actually.

LUCILLE: Are you a transfer from the Connecticut Exchange?

JUNE: This is my first day on the job.

LUCILLE: Did they tell you this is where Protestants come to retire? You put twenty miserable years in on that wadded up snot rag of an island kingdom of yours then you want to come to mine? Why? Because they've got the Blacks to pick the cotton? That's down South baby. And the Chinese to build the railroads? Well that's out West darling. And Italians to bring you ice? Maybe baby. Maybe not. 'You won't have to lift a finger,' they said. 'It's paradise for Protestants,' they said. 'The mongrels fall over themselves to curry favor,' they said. Didn't expect this did you? (*Pause.*) Does it look like what you imagined hell would look like? I only wish you'd arrived on one of our sunny days. You might have melted. We've got sunny days don't we Pippa? I think New York might be hell for Protestants.

JUNE: I noticed.

LUCILLE: Heh?

JUNE: I said I noticed.

LUCILLE: Noticed what?

JUNE: It's fast out there. And very loud. Everything moves quickly. And it seems to get faster every time I visit.

LUCILLE: Oh yeah, I wouldn't know.

JUNE: Faster every day even. Did I do something to offend you?

LUCILLE: Be born in England to start. Sat next to me in addition. Talked back for a cherry on top.

JUNE: I won't argue the relative merits of our respective countries. England doesn't need me to defend her.

LUCILLE: Who?

JUNE: England. If that's what you meant.

LUCILLE: Always knew 'he' was a 'she'.

JUNE: It's an expression.

LUCILLE: I've heard of those.

TRUMAN: Lu?

LUCILLE: Have you got designs on me Truman? Because I can't seem to pull you out of my crack this morning.

TRUMAN: I'm just –

LUCILLE: I was just training the new girl. Teaching her about our battle to destroy time.

TRUMAN: Maybe you should start with the error codes Lucille.

PHILIPPA: How do you like New York?

LUCILLE: Excuse me Pippa, I am in the middle of training the new girl.

PHILIPPA: Says you! I'm trying to be friendly, you ought to try it some time.

JUNE: It's a lovely city, thank you for asking.

Pause.

Different than I expected. But I've been in the United States for some while. I was a seamstress during the war.

LUCILLE: Seamstress huh? I don't know anything about clothes. Me? I don't really see clothes. I see men who miss feathers. I see women who miss their fur. That's New York. Primitive, bambino, unchanging. That's the immigrant's advantage: We remember the world before America, before America created time. Created this thing time in its own image and cast it from the Garden. Time is their boogeyman, they want us to destroy it for them. They make the Chinese fight distance. Make the Jews fight the brain and the planets. And here we are doing our duty, chopping up time. Make no mistake we are soldiers in America's army, fighting her war against Time. I maintain that the enemy is fabricated, but she is a worthy nemesis none-the-less.

JUNE: I think your analysis of the situation is very astute.

LUCILLE: Your queen won't have prepared you for this. She only gave you two nostrils. She only gave you ten fingertips. You've only got one tongue. And what does your tongue know? Your tongue knows a fish from a potato. You'll hardly know where to begin in New York so impoverished are your poor senses. And forget about your ears. Go ahead and memorize the complaint codes, it'll take you a day. Your ears won't mature for seven years. You're like a wet chicky. You've got little holes full of snot where your ears hope to grow. And worst of all you don't speak English. You might know the rules of grammar but you don't speak it. You don't remember how, or never learned. Too many conversations with God squatting in some Protestant hovel. You've been raised by dogs, but you can't hear their frequencies. I hear the frequencies only dogs hear. This is why I have headaches and need my medicine.

LUCILLE finishes her drink.

No. She's all yours. Truman?

TRUMAN: Yes thank you Lucille. Okay. There's actually a poem I like to read to the new girls. Sort of an inspiration.

JUNE: If it's all the same to you Truman I'd like to get on with the training.

TRUMAN: I didn't write it. Merlan Berry published it in 'Telephony' a few years –

JUNE: If it's all the same, Truman. I promise.

TRUMAN: Okay. It's Mr Ashdor. I prefer Mr Ashdor.

JUNE: I'm sorry.

For a moment it seems as if JUNE might cry, overwhelmed.

TRUMAN: No, it's alright.

JUNE: It's fine.

TRUMAN: Maybe later.

Pause.

The poem.

JUNE: Yes please.

TRUMAN: Truman's fine.

JUNE: Mr Ashdor.

TRUMAN: Suit yourself.

TRUMAN and JUNE trade small, hesitant smiles.

PHILIPPA: (*Suddenly, frantically.*) No. No. No. Stop. Alright stop. Mac I read you you gotta slow down so I can get the address. Tell me again.

Short pause.

East sixth? Calm down Mac I'm going to send 'em right over. Don't sweat it they'll be there in a jiffy. I promise Mac. (*PHILIPPA is suddenly frantically connecting and disconnecting lines.*) Damnit. It's a fire.

ANDREW: Where?

PHILIPPA: Local 82? This is Philippa at the Public Library Exchange. I need you down to 6th and Mercer they've got a blaze going down there sounds serious. Alright, good luck. Does it...no go ahead I'm sorry.

She hangs up suddenly and nearly dives into her drawer for extra candy.

Geez that was dark! He was hollerin' like something awful. He might have been crying. He was a big six fella too, deep voice, cracking up into the line. God.

ANDREW: Was he in it?

PHILIPPA: I could barely get the address out of him.

ANDREW: Well. Lucky it's raining.

PHILIPPA: Oh pipe down will you?

ANDREW: I'm trying to calm you down! What's a fire when it's raining this hard?

PHILIPPA: Well if they've got a roof it's a fire like any other fire.

ANDREW: Don't call the subscribers 'Mac' alright? This isn't a goddamn speakeasy.

PHILIPPA: Oh LAY OFF will you? You could eat fire and no one would believe you were hard nut Ethel. You ain't foolin' anyone.

ANDREW: This isn't a dormitory Pippa, put your goddamn shoes on.

PHILIPPA: Why don't you come over here and scientifically manage the lousy shoes onto my feet if you've got the stones?

LUCILLE: Local 82's near Mercer Pip. They'll get there quick. It'll be fine.

PHILIPPA: (*Still mostly to ANDREW.*) That's my neighborhood.

LUCILLE: I know doll. It won't spread in this rain though, that much is certain. Not to your mom's crib.

PHILIPPA: I know.

LUCILLE: Have another candy.

PHILIPPA: Yeah. Thanks Lu.

LUCILLE: That's anything for you Pippa, truly.

LUCILLE and PHILIPPA's boards ring simultaneously. LUCILLE turns as if to answer but returns with her bottle to pour herself another. PHILIPPA, exasperated, answers the line. TRUMAN is back to training JUNE.

TRUMAN: Half the job is these complaint reports and they're real strict about it so it's worth memorizing. They can dock you for aberrant phrasing but the subscribers never complain about that, they usually appreciate a personal touch. You didn't hear that from me. The matrons are always griping about the exact wording but I'm more of a stickler about the tone of it. Always going up on the questions? (*TRUMAN phrases it like a questions by way of demonstration.*) And enunciating the numbers. Enunciating the numbers will save you lots of complaint reports, some of the upper west side types hate to repeat themselves.

Pause.

I mean it. It's their least favorite thing to do. God knows why.

Pause.

Anyway, productivity is the big thing and these abbreviations are going to save you time. The chief won't sign your slips if you don't abbreviate because they'll just make her do it and manual says it's your job. And all the clerks know that.

Pause.

Actually I'll probably be signing most of your complaint forms, either myself or Andrew, so just do us the favor? Okay. Let's try some of these. So how about a double C?

JUNE: 'Can't connect'?

TRUMAN: 'Can't call'. Sort of the same thing. C.O?

JUNE: 'Call – .' Um. 'Called Operator'? No, that's me.

TRUMAN: 'Cuts Out.' That's when they specify that the line is choppy. It 'cuts out'. That's usually specific, though. They'll usually just say 'bad connection' which is – ?

JUNE: B.C.?

TRUMAN: B.C.N. actually. That was close. 'B.C.' is the Boston College Exchange so we have a...

JUNE: Okay. B.C.N.

TRUMAN: B.D.R.?

JUNE: Bell don't ring?

TRUMAN: Correct. There are only twenty-one common complaint codes.

JUNE: Oh good.

LUCILLE: 'Oh good,' she says. I don't think you were built for this Dora.

TRUMAN: W.C.F?

JUNE: I don't know.

LUCILLE: 'Wire Chief.'

TRUMAN: Right, that's –

LUCILLE: That's 'your man' Truman, a poetry-loving family man with a heavy heart and an even heavier wife, but he loves her just the same, doesn't he?

JUNE: We've already made our introductions.

TRUMAN: You said my wife was pretty.

PHILIPPA: Oh your wife's a tomato, there's no doubt.

TRUMAN: A what?

LUCILLE: I think it's good.

PHILIPPA: What? Yeah! That's good Truman. A tomato's a fox.

LUCILLE: She's a looker Truman.

ANDREW: She's a teetotaler!

TRUMAN: Well you just said –

LUCILLE: I like 'em big Truman. You and I have a few things in common. Truman's your wire chief. I'm your C.F.

Pause.

JUNE: It's my first day.

LUCILLE: 'Chief Operator'. Owing to my seniority and general excellence, not to mention a kind of legendary status to rival that of any Hollywood starlet along with the requisite grace, on account of how much I get around on the wires and such. You listening to me?

TRUMAN: Tricky one: X.D.?

JUNE: (*To TRUMAN.*) 'Crossed' – (*To LUCILLE.*) Am I listening to you? Is there anything else to be done when you speak?

LUCILLE: Give me your attention and you might learn something.

JUNE: I gather attention is something you'd rather take than be given. Or maybe you don't know the difference.

LUCILLE: Are you calling me a thief?

JUNE: Actually I'm calling you thoughtless, which is much worse.

LUCILLE: Thoughtless? Don't you mean insensitive? I got no shortage of thoughts.

JUNE: Take it how you want it.

LUCILLE: I don't know any other way to take it.

TRUMAN: Did you study that one?

JUNE: WHAT?

TRUMAN: X.D. You're right. It's the code for 'crossed'. That's a tricky one. Did you study it?

JUNE: (*After a pause.*) Lucky guess.

TRUMAN: Lucky guess?

JUNE: I studied a bit.

LUCILLE: Maybe she's a witch. Heh? Pippa? Witch.

PHILIPPA: Speak!

LUCILLE: Demand!

PHILIPPA: We'll answer!

LUCILLE: Right Truman?

TRUMAN: I get it okay? My wife told me what it's from.

LUCILLE: Keep mentioning her and I won't get a thing done today.

ANDREW: (*Handing a newspaper to PHILIPPA.*) Look at this.

PHILIPPA: Oh I know it.

ANDREW: So why are they bringing in new girls?

PHILIPPA: I don't know.

ANDREW: Must be good news.

PHILIPPA: It?

ANDREW: No. Her. (*Indicating JUNE.*)

PHILIPPA: Maybe.

TRUMAN: Hey! What's that?

ANDREW: Nothing. Menu. Breakfast!

ANDREW exits to collect brown paper packages with breakfast for the operators.

TRUMAN: What time is it?

ANDREW: Don't worry. I've got it today. You carry on.

A mechanical roar is again heard from backstage.

TRUMAN: Hold on. (*To JUNE.*) Why don't you take the break with the rest of them. It'll take you a while to get used to the hours.

TRUMAN follows ANDREW offstage as ANDREW reenters and begins tossing the brown-bag-breakfasts to the girls. He throws first to JUNE, then LUCILLE, then PHILIPPA.

ANDREW: (*With the throwing.*) Pippa! Lu! New girl! Bone appa teet.

Immediately after catching their bags LUCILLE and PHILIPPA take aim and pitch their bags into a nearby garbage pail which has, until now, been collecting rain water.

PHILIPPA: (*If LUCILLE makes her shot.*) Murder! (*If LUCILLE misses, in a baseball announcer voices.*) She's no Eddie Cicotte.

LUCILLE: I retired my spitball like a good girl. (*To PHILIPPA.*) Wha'd ya bring?

JUNE stares into her bag, confused.

PHILIPPA: I thought it was your turn?

LUCILLE: My turn?! What my turn? I brought that goddamn svigliadel yesterday you lazy WASP good-for-nothing. What the hell am I going to eat?

PHILIPPA: Just kidding. I brought sinkers.

She produces a box of doughnuts.

LUCILLE: Mmm. Need milk. Ethel! Milk!

She pulls out a bottle of vodka, pours the vodka into a mug and begins dunking her doughnut in the alcohol.

ANDREW: I can't hear you.

PHILIPPA: (*To JUNE.*) Don't eat that doll. It's poison.

JUNE: Is it ham?

PHILIPPA: Ham without a memory of the pig from which it came. Want a sinker?

LUCILLE: (*Mouth full of doughnut.*) How many are left?

PHILIPPA: Relax, I got a box, geez!

LUCILLE: Give her a plain one, I hate the plain.

PHILIPPA: I'm giving her a powder. (*She does.*)

JUNE: Thank you.

LUCILLE: (*To JUNE.*) Do you want a drink?

Pause.

JUNE: It isn't even nine yet.

LUCILLE: Right. It's after six. After six is the rule. What time is it?

ANDREW: Seven-forty.

LUCILLE: You're fine!

PHILIPPA: Lu, it's seven-forty in the morning.

LUCILLE: Is it?

JUNE: Yes. (*She bites her doughnut.*)

Pause.

LUCILLE: Dannazione e un lever del sole perpetuo.

JUNE: (*Expressing that the doughnut tastes good.*) Mmmmm.

PHILIPPA: Berries right?

JUNE: Hm?

PHILIPPA: It's the berries.

JUNE: Mine's just powder.

PHILIPPA: I mean it's good.

JUNE: It is good.

PHILIPPA: I get 'em from a Dutch fella on Bleecker. Half a clam gets you twelve, vamp and he'll toss in two more.

JUNE: Vamp?

LUCILLE: 'Flirt.' Pippa's a whore. It's true.

PHILIPPA: Whore for cheap sinkers. Guilty.

LUCILLE: How do the advantages of marriage stand against our freedom to flirt for cheap sinkers?

PHILIPPA: Oh marriage. The only men I talk to are these business squares.

LUCILLE: Our subscribers are captains of industry, men about town, wheeler-dealers; you'd be smart to cuddle up on one of those squares.

PHILIPPA: Not my type.

LUCILLE: 'Not your type.' Stop. You gonna go half on a brat with 'jazz cat'? Please.

PHILIPPA: I don't crush on musicians. I like a hard-nut. A dock-worker. Money doesn't matter to me.

LUCILLE: Dock-workers? With their rakishly tilted wooly hats? With their impeccably scuffed boots? Dock-workers don't fool me. 'Money doesn't matter to me.' Please.

PHILIPPA: Some of them are probably quite gentle.

LUCILLE: Some of them? All of them. All of them are 'quite gentle.' They're cupcakes the lot. Imposters to masculinity.

PHILIPPA: Dock-workers?

LUCILLE: Dock-workers.

JUNE: The men who work the ship-yards come from very good stock.

LUCILLE: (*To JUNE.*) It's much different in New York. (*To PHILIPPA.*) And half the fish-mongers.

PHILIPPA: They look tough enough to me.

JUNE: Half the fish-mongers what?

LUCILLE: Cupcakes. The lot!

PHILIPPA: I'm an old-fashioned girl. I think they're old-fashioned.

LUCILLE: First of all: What does that mean? Second of all: No they're not. They're new fashioned. New-fangled if you will? I will, will you? Thank you. 'Fangled.' Mark that, it's mine.

PHILIPPA: Yeah, I'll 'mark' that.

LUCILLE: Don't act cross.

PHILIPPA: Not acting.

LUCILLE: Don't you dare be cross.

PHILIPPA: I want a real man, that's my style.

LUCILLE: Not a dock-worker honey. They're communists. That isn't sexy.

PHILIPPA: It is to me. You're always ruining everything for me.

LUCILLE: I'm helping you.

PHILIPPA: They're not all communists.

LUCILLE: The snazzy, old-fashioned-looking ones are.

PHILIPPA: What do you know about men anyway?

LUCILLE: Bite your tongue.

PHILIPPA: You don't even care for men, what kind of advice can you possibly –

LUCILLE: What? What about the six years I gave to my husband God rest?

PHILIPPA: You weren't married.

LUCILLE: I was!

PHILIPPA: What was his name?

LUCILLE: Oh who knows. It is was only six years.

JUNE: Is your husband dead?

LUCILLE: (*Short pause.*) Good as. Who would know the difference anyway. Half the day in cafes with coffee, by two he was at the bars with drink. The city swallowed that turd. Goodbye. Dorma in pace. (*She drinks.*) Bold question. You'll make a good friend to Pippa for the next twenty minutes as she pretends to hate me. (*Drinks again.*) More milk!

JUNE: Is this how you support yourself then?

LUCILLE: Milk! Milk! I need it for my goddamn bones! They've stopped growing! Milk!

ANDREW: What are you hollering about?

LUCILLE: MILK!

ANDREW: There is milk in your bag.

LUCILLE: What bag?

ANDREW: Where's your bag?

JUNE: That was milk? (*JUNE reaches into her bag.*)

LUCILLE: What? Lemme see.

ANDREW: It's you two been throwing away your breakfast in the goddamn refuse bin? I thought it was the Jewish girls on account of the ham. That's a goddamn waste.

JUNE has pulled a small carton of milk from her bag.

PHILIPPA: In a box?

LUCILLE: Throw it here.

JUNE tosses it to LUCILLE, who reaches to catch it and misses by about two feet and a full second. The box slides over to PHILIPPA.

Never mind. Pippa, you open it.

PHILIPPA: (*Picking up the carton.*) It'll go sour in half a second in a box.

ANDREW: No, there's wax on the cardboard.

PHILIPPA: (*Sniffs and shakes the carton.*) I'm not trusting this.

LUCILLE: Give it.

PHILIPPA: Keep your eyeball on the ball here.

LUCILLE: Give it!

> *PHILIPPA throws it. LUCILLE catches it this time. She shakes and sniffs it.*

No: This is good.

PHILIPPA: Taste it.

LUCILLE: I'm not afraid to taste it.

ANDREW: It's called a Pure-Pak.

PHILIPPA: Why you hovering? Your daddy invent the goddamn thing?

ANDREW: I'm interested in science.

> *Pause.*

PHILIPPA: It ain't science. It's engineering.

ANDREW: So smart.

JUNE: I've never seen anything like it.

PHILIPPA: Right. 'Cause you drink tea over there.

JUNE: The box I mean.

LUCILLE: I declare this milk to be of the highest quality. Delicious, cold, and unpolluted.

ANDREW: Well, the cold is because I keep them in an ice-box in the –

LUCILLE: I declare the card-board-boxing of milk –

ANDREW: Pure-Pak.

LUCILLE: – to be the greatest technological innovation since Monsieur Louis Pasteur discovered, and in turn clobbered, the germ.

PHILIPPA: Oh, you're blotto, you wouldn't know if it's fresh or sour.

LUCILLE: Fresh? What's fresh? Fresh from the cow? I don't want fresh. You'll find me in a Chinatown dumpster before I would drink 'fresh' milk from an udder. Wash the chicken off my eggs! Wash from my eggs the memory of a chicken's vagina.

PHILIPPA: Lucille!

LUCILLE: I genuinely hate farmers. I genuinely do. And the rhythms of nature.

Pause.

I will admit to being intimidated by insects, but only when I encounter them on their own turf. I'll give them that. May I propose a toast?

PHILIPPA: Not with that milk you ain't.

LUCILLE: Give me your glasses, you're both going to have a drink with me.

PHILIPPA: Lu, I can't get zozzled before lunch. Not on a Monday.

LUCILLE: What zozzled? Quit it with the goddamn jazz jargon. If that means drunk, you won't get 'zozzled'.

PHILIPPA: If it's that coffin varnish you drink I'll get drunk off the fumes.

LUCILLE: Really Pippa, there are ladies present for whom normal English ain't even our first language.

JUNE: I'll have a drink.

PHILIPPA gets up and pours a drink for JUNE, then herself.
LUCILLE pours vodka into her milk carton. ANDREW steps up
and fills a glass.

LUCILLE: See now that's class. She didn't get off on the right
foot, now she's going to make amends by partaking in one of
the local customs of our foreign culture.

PHILIPPA: It isn't a local custom if you're the only one doing it.

LUCILLE: I'm my own local.

TRUMAN re-enters. His sleeves are rolled up. ANDREW raises a
glass to toast him.

I would like to propose a toast: To the –

TRUMAN: What's this?

LUCILLE: Interrupting.

TRUMAN: Sorry.

LUCILLE: I would like to propose a toast: To the bleeding heart
of Christ, the Bell Atlantic Telephone Company, and our holy
Pope Benedict the Fifteenth though he is, in my opinion, no
Pius the Tenth.

JUNE lowers her drink slightly.

Bless the scars on the tops of our heads and the cuts on the
bottoms of our feet Lord. Lord. God bless the fishnets. God
bless hot loaves from the oven. God bless buns in the oven.
God bless the twin trout and the troubled forest of sin. Cheers.

LUCILLE and PHILIPPA knock back the drinks in one shot.
JUNE sips about half her drink. PHILIPPA makes a pained
expression and holds it.

JUNE: That's very strong.

LUCILLE: Nah. Wait until Prohibition.

JUNE: Prohibition?

LUCILLE: I'm with the Prods on that one. Hands down. They've got my vote.

JUNE: You're in favor of prohibition?

LUCILLE: I say bring it on. Believe me, nothing kicks harder than bathtub booze.

JUNE: It'll be us drinking the bathtub booze. Not them.

LUCILLE: Essattamente. Addesso, tu capisci!

PHILIPPA: I'm drunk.

LUCILLE: You're not drunk, for Christ's sake!

PHILIPPA either begins to giggle uncontrollably or buries her head in her hands.

My God, how can you be drunk already. You have the constitution of a six year old child!

TRUMAN: Alright listen. I've got an announcement to make.

LUCILLE: Truman have a drink.

TRUMAN: I won't have a drink. I'm not drinking anymore Lucille, and out of respect for me, I'd appreciate it if you'd do the same.

LUCILLE: These Protestants, they have no church, so they worship in their homes, they try to improve their lives, they make 'progress', which I believe is the worst play I've ever seen: 'Human Progress.'

PHILIPPA: What? Who's a Protestant.

TRUMAN: I've given up drink.

ANDREW: His wife is making him.

TRUMAN: It's not just my wife!

ANDREW: I'm his sponsor.

TRUMAN: (*To ANDREW.*) This affects you too.

ANDREW: I told you I'm not quitting.

TRUMAN: The announcement!

ANDREW: What announcement?

Pause.

Oh. Alright, listen up girls.

PHILIPPA: (*To JUNE.*) Did he touch your ass, when he was measuring you?

JUNE: What?

TRUMAN: Excuse me.

PHILIPPA: Touch. Your ass. When he was 'measuring' you.

TRUMAN: Pippa.

PHILIPPA: He did it to me too.

ANDREW: Is she drunk?

LUCILLE: Well, I can't fault you Ethel, I'd have done the same.

JUNE: He didn't. Maybe with his elbow, when he was measuring my waist.

PHILIPPA: Oh, you measure waists now?

ANDREW: We always do!

PHILIPPA: Progress. My day they just pawed your ass, there was no Hail Mary move to cover it up.

JUNE: (*To ANDREW.*) You fucking pig.

TRUMAN: Whoa!

ANDREW: (*To PHILIPPA.*) Look at you, you're completely drunk.

PHILIPPA: I am drunk!

LUCILLE: You're not drunk.

ANDREW: (*To JUNE.*) I didn't touch anything.

JUNE: I thought so! Twenty minutes to take measurements and you keep forgetting the numbers and re-doing them. And you're management!

TRUMAN: He's sorry.

ANDREW: I'm not!

TRUMAN: I'm trying to make the announcement.

ANDREW: Good, tell them.

JUNE: Bloody fucking hell.

TRUMAN: Jesus Christ.

ANDREW: You're all fired. That's the announcement. Pack it up. Bell is switching to the Strowger. (*To TRUMAN.*) Strowager? Strowger.

TRUMAN: Strowger.

ANDREW: It's the automatic model.

LUCILLE: Of what?

ANDREW: Of you.

TRUMAN: It's not. We're not. We're talking to Automatic Electric. They're talking to A.E. in Chicago.

Long pause.

PHILIPPA: What? (*Pause. Looks at ANDREW.*) But they hired a new girl. Why did they hire a new girl then.

ANDREW: So it's short-term employment for her. She just waiting to catch a man anyway.

LUCILLE: Strowger?

JUNE: Did you hear what he just said?

LUCILLE: How come I never heard of this thing?

JUNE: You lied to me.

TRUMAN: It's a trial. There's a bottle-neck.

LUCILLE: Bottle-neck?

TRUMAN: Not here. Not yet. But there are more subscribers everyday. They want to put phones in every home.

ANDREW: And anyway these things run on simple electricity. They don't require liquid fuel. That means they run quieter and it's easier to clean up after them.

ANDREW dumps the contents of one of LUCILLE's liquor bottles into the trashcan, then overturns the trash onto the stage...

PHILIPPA: Andrew?

ANDREW: Yes?

LUCILLE: A bottle-neck.

PHILIPPA: Did you ever indulge yourself, may I ask, with a hot bun on a cold day somewhere on the busy streets of New York? Did you? Did you eat it? Did you lend a helping hand to a man in need? How many hands did you lend? How many did you lend? How many pulled you Andrew?

There is a sudden and complete power-outage in the exchange office. The only light is a very dim glow directly above LUCILLE's head.

TRUMAN: Crap.

ANDREW: What's this?

TRUMAN: It's the rain. Goddamn brown-out.

LUCILLE: A bottle-neck.

LUCILLE incants a Catholic Italian blessing, then slowly, in the darkness and quiet, like a sermon:

The corpus, that is Latin for 'body', is made of chemicals. And it possesses an uncanny.

Pause.

Not uncanny.

She slurps her drink.

An altogether average capacity for adaptations to foreign bodies and vicious liquids. Be kind bevil.

She slurps again, and pours more.

JUNE: I have something to tell you when you get a moment. This isn't my first day on the job.

LUCILLE: In San Antonio they know the sound of my voice and I will die, certainly, having never experienced the feeling of hot sand between my toes. But in San Antonio they know the sound of my voice.

LUCILLE drops a bottle or knocks over a glass.

TRUMAN: Everybody just sit tight.

JUNE: Lucille?

TRUMAN and ANDREW are banging around the stage.

LUCILLE: It is remarkable how one experiences the stimulations of life when the body is no boundary. That is: unmoored, unchained from flesh the voice wanders places the toes may never touch. The mind goes where fingers won't fit, and I pity the fool – mark that it's mine – I pity the fool, and there are many, whose skin is like a prophylactic shielding them from the orgy of sensation this world puts on offer. Not physical sensation. That's no good. If you are bored, look no further than the body for a culprit, for it is our bodies, the whole range from clumsy and bloated to lean and graceful which interrupt our relationship with the world.

Pause.

Crafty flesh. It gives us farts of joy and we are satisfied...there. Tricky body. The voice, the mind, the imagination, with these tools we may know this world completely, from any angle, in any manner, but most are addicted to the squirt and clutch of the body. You don't fool me. I will overcome my body. It is a horse to be beaten, a child to be molested and discarded. I respect only the dogged dignity of my liver, the rest can leave at sunrise without a kiss. This life is a one-night stand with a cheap whore: the body. I am holding out for my marriage to Christ.

Pause.

A bottleneck.

Pause.

That you would design to replace this voice, this mind, this spirit, with a machine, is a sacrilege. It is an affront to Christendom. You may hate our poor bodies, as do I. You may resent our stutters, our addictions, our arthritic teeth and rotten muscles, you may condemn our habits and our sins, but you must forgive them! As Christ did, you must also do. Otherwise this corporation will be demolished by an angry, vengeful God, who does not accept the profit margin as an adequate excuse for replacing human beings with soulless automatons! (*She drinks.*) I say soulless automatons! The Strowger!

JUNE: (*Whispering.*) I have something to tell you.

Pause.

I represent the Union.

Pause.

We want to help you.

LUCILLE: Who can help?

JUNE: Shhhhh. The Union can help you.

The curtain closes slowly. End of Act One.

Act Two

Curtain opens. The power has been restored, but there are a few lit candles scattered throughout the office. LUCILLE's back is facing the audience, open beer bottle in her hand. Her switchboard has been removed from the office. She is still wearing her headset and microphone, and her voice is amplified. JUNE is seated stage left in PHILIPPA's chair which is now approximately two feet downstage of LUCILLE's chair. PHILIPPA is passed out on the floor. The stage left switchboard has been replaced with a Strowger Automated Switching System. TRUMAN is struggling to hook up the Strowger by himself.

JUNE: I hate this city. I'll admit it. I hate all the secrets. I hate the new words for things and no one cares if you learn them. I hate going into shops and feeling like I'm an intruder. An intruder on their kingdom, the chemists! The bodega, or whatever it is. Petty local despots pimping sandwiches. And nobody has any shame. They don't care if you see them, they want you to see them. And crowded! Stumble in front of a bus stop and you've got fifteen people laughing at you like they paid admission. Or not laughing, and they paid admission. Even worse. And the general loneliness. That ain't right. Nobody sees me. I know if I died, in the street, struck down from or by whatever, I wouldn't be me! I'd be a traffic jam. My corpse wouldn't be a story about me, it'd be a story about New York. And how brutal it is. And how dangerous it is. And how exciting it is. 'Only in New York.' My living end. 'Only in New York.' Yes.

Pause.

I know why New York hates the union. Solidarity terrifies you doesn't it? You don't trust anyone! I can see why.
So, yes! I take a paycheck from the Union to undo the dirt done by these tycoons. The aforementioned tycoons. Our enemy. For the gentlewomen and ladies assembled here and

across your Republic. This is my work so I can hardly be faulted my subterfuge. I'm the good hands into which you should place your best interests, best intentions, and trust.

ANDREW: Whose best interests?

JUNE: I think you'd be surprised. You'd be surprised to hear how much it has to do with proximity. The girls close to headquarters tend to rally around management – feel uncomfortable taking a stand when the higher-ups are just down the road.

Pause.

I think you've spent too much time in the city. There is a recourse apart from corruption you know. It's Labor Organization.

Pause.

It isn't a question of whether you will be replaced Lucille. Every trade magazine is rammed with ads for 'girl-less, gossip-less service', not to mention letters from business owners accusing operators of redirecting calls in exchange for cash.

Pause.

There is a country west of the Hudson River Lucille, and they don't share your nostalgia for the bad old days.

ANDREW: In whose best interests? Really? Tell her.

JUNE: It isn't illegal for women to organize their labor Andrew. It isn't illegal to organize against redundancy.

ANDREW: Redundancy redundancy redundancy.

Pause.

Get it?

JUNE: Honestly, I didn't expect your cooperation Andrew. No need to poison the well, the rest can make up their own damn minds.

ANDREW: You've got a lot of nerve. Touched your ass. Whose ass?

JUNE: Ah. (*Disappointed.*) You are forgiven your indiscretions. I can't speak for Philippa.

PHILIPPA: (*From the floor.*) Ha? Wha?

ANDREW: Really? Am I forgiven my indiscretions? But how would that work? Explain my indiscretions to me. Because I didn't touch the ass of any Union representative. I didn't touch the ass of any spy-trouble-maker come all the way across the Atlantic to teach us how to conduct our free enterprise. I didn't touch the ass of some two-face Trojan whore. I touched the ass of a big-eyed cuddler first day on the job trying to make friends. And she isn't here anymore. So I believe I am absolved by default, owing to the fact that the big-eyed cuddler never existed in the first place. Any ass I touched was a cruel illusion. So I believe I am absolved by default.

JUNE: I'm sorry you're offended.

ANDREW: I am offended.

JUNE: Let's put it behind us.

ANDREW: I'm not falling for that again.

JUNE produces from her pocket an advertisement clipped from Telephony *magazine. It is an advertisement for the Strowger Automatic Telephone System*

JUNE: 'You, Your Subscriber, and The Dial.' That's what the advertisements say. 'You, Your Subscriber, and The Dial.' You (*Pointing to ANDREW.*) Not us. You. Your – You – Your subscriber. And the dial. And isn't this advertisement just filthy with Her absence. Doesn't Her absence just fill the room. It is an extraordinary absence. And, finally, it is a question of whether or not we will fight. And how can you refuse the fight? You can't. So you organize your labor.

ANDREW: So what's in it for me?

TRUMAN: Andrew?

ANDREW: What?

TRUMAN has been struggling with the Strowger by himself.

TRUMAN: Help me.

ANDREW: In a minute.

JUNE: We must exert our absence before the company does. Exert our absence before Bell Atlantic does it for us. You attack the thing which the corporation loves most.

ANDREW: What?

JUNE: Today's profit. Attack the day's profit and even the shrewdest tycoon will momentarily forget about his long-term dividends. It's happening in the western states. It's happening in the southern states. It is a pre-emptive, profit-attacking absence.

ANDREW: What is?

JUNE: A walkout.

LUCILLE: Ha!

ANDREW grabs the advertisement from JUNE.

ANDREW: But it says 'you', meaning me! And then 'your', meaning my, subscriber. It's a promise to me. I'm not angry about this. This is cause for celebration. Right Truman?

TRUMAN: Are you going to help me?

ANDREW: Well, no celebration for Truman, but it's wonderful news just the same.

JUNE: You trust those men upstairs? Let me ask you a question? Do you trust your sex?

ANDREW: Go ahead, they call me 'Ethel' and 'Nancy' all day, that noise goes in one ear and out the other.

JUNE: I doubt you are guaranteed any job security whatsoever.

ANDREW: Well, looks like they're going to chop the tits off this corporation first so I guess it doesn't fucking matter.

ANDREW gives JUNE the finger.

Pause.

LUCILLE: You want us to sign up with you?

JUNE: Thank you! Yes, you must. It's just a matter of whether the gentlemen trust their brothers in high places to feed them tomorrow. Pippa, wake up please.

TRUMAN: Wait.

TRUMAN flips a switch and the Strowger automatic switchboard lights up as if alive. It has many little lights which flash and blink. It is intimidating.

There we go.

ANDREW: (*To JUNE.*) It's shit.

TRUMAN: Hey!

TRUMAN gestures toward the board as if it might be impolite to curse in front of it; as if it is an innocent child that mustn't be corrupted.

ANDREW: It's cock-eyed. Organize our labor? Into what? Like what? It's a cock-a-mammy idea. (*ANDREW sees the Strowger all lit up.*) Look, you did it yourself. You didn't need my help.

TRUMAN: Yeah, I must have really miscalculated there.

ANDREW: You did.

JUNE: Truman, get Pippa up will you. Pippa's on our side, isn't she Pippa?

TRUMAN goes to pick PHILIPPA off the floor. She is drunk, but speaks clearly without slurring. Her body is completely limp.

TRUMAN: (*To PHILIPPA.*) Are you drunk?

PHILIPPA: Darling, do I look drunk?

JUNE: She's fine.

PHILIPPA: This ain't drunk. Really I'm just very tired. And I barely ate anything, so that little nip I took just went straight to bed.

JUNE: Pippa darling you've got to wake up. You're missing everything.

PHILIPPA: Straight to bed. So I'll just. You know. Finish napping and after lunch, you and me Truman.

TRUMAN: It's almost three.

PHILIPPA: Just you and me Truman. A night on the town.

LUCILLE: Easy Truman.

TRUMAN: No, what? It has nothing to do with me.

PHILIPPA: You and I can blow this hot-dog eating contest and have a few high-balls in the Rainbow Room. We can have prime-rib at a well-lit Times Square bistro.

TRUMAN: Okay, none of that for me unfortunately.

PHILIPPA: Give me five more minutes and we'll have a dance.

TRUMAN: Well, there's certainly nothing wrong with that. No problem. But let's just use our legs now. Go ahead. A little walking.

PHILIPPA: Two minutes. I'll dance with you in two minutes.

TRUMAN: She thinks I'm someone else.

PHILIPPA: Oh Truman.

JUNE: Alright, damnit, put her down!

TRUMAN ceases his struggle to keep her upright and puts her back down on the floor.

TRUMAN: I'm a married man. Okay?

JUNE: Fine. Lucille, she'll be up in a moment, and I'm positive she's up for a walkout.

LUCILLE: How did I never hear anything about this Strowger?

JUNE: That's precisely my point Lucille. I doubt you know anything about this machine. You haven't a clue what you're up against.

LUCILLE: I think I've got a pretty good idea of what I'm up against. Fifty pounds give or take. Knickerbocker Avenue rules. We can make it happen.

TRUMAN: No. This thing was heavy. Much heavier than you.

LUCILLE: Naturally. What I meant.

TRUMAN: Oh.

JUNE: Excuse me. I'm not sure what kind of ridiculous mixed cocktail you've been drinking or breathing or God knows what you do with it, but the Cat is out of the Bag here. A thousand ships have sailed and yours is hardly the face. This is early retirement before the weekend for us. This is pink-slip Thursday if you don't make a stand – take a stand! – right now.

LUCILLE: I don't scare easy.

JUNE: Scare easier darling or find yourself a husband. That or a street corner upon which needle packs for a dime and pencils ten for a quarter. That's door number three in case you're counting.

ANDREW: Door number three?

JUNE: Mark that, it's mine.

LUCILLE: Drinks my liquor.

JUNE: Anyway, it's not you I'm worried about. If you can manage to pull your tongue out of that bottle for a fortnight you could become a bootlegging tycoon. It's the others I'm worried about, without purpose or recourse – No net and no retirement plan. As I say.

ANDREW: I'm telling you to speak for yourself. My team isn't getting pink-slipped unless I hear about it from upstairs.

TRUMAN: Your team?

ANDREW: Oh, come off it Truman, what are you? Two months off of retirement? Three months?

TRUMAN: I'm fifty-two!

ANDREW: All of a sudden Sonny Boy wants the job!

TRUMAN: Want the job? I don't have to want it Andrew, it's mine!

ANDREW: Are you a fucking sap or what huh? It's 'yours'? You can't even keep these birds sober for a half a shift.

TRUMAN: I let you drink too.

ANDREW: You're unfit to govern. I'm taking your job.

TRUMAN: You've been here two years.

ANDREW: So what? I know Franklin upstairs.

TRUMAN: Who's Franklin?

ANDREW: You want to organize these clowns? Truman doesn't know his boss's Christian name. Organize their labor? Why don't you see if any of them even remember to cash their paychecks. As a matter of fact, I'm not even sure if everyone in the room is still an employee of Bell Atlantic. I suspect it might just be that the bosses haven't been through the office in a few years. I know for a fact that Pippa's the only operator I ever heard got fired and never picked up her pink slip. After two months they just put her back on the payroll.

TRUMAN: Alright, I've had it. Listen everyone. Listen Lucille, this is the last of me. I'm fucking had it.

LUCILLE: Now you with the mouth too? It's greedy.

TRUMAN: Everything is out of control. Everything is out of control and now I'm going to bring it under control. First off, someone wake Pippa up right now, she's passed out for crying-out-loud.

ANDREW moves.

Not you, you need to hear the rest of what I'm saying. And you two stay seated because I got – (*TRUMAN sees that neither LUCILLE nor JUNE have moved at all.*) – Alright. I'm not good at speeches. But this is important.

ANDREW: Well if it's that important don't you want Pippa to hear it?

TRUMAN: It doesn't matter. Do you think it matters? It doesn't – Yes, wake her up. Hold on. Fresh start.

ANDREW picks PHILIPPA up and drags her into a chair. JUNE's board rings and she moves to answer it.

Goddamnit. No. Everything is – hurry up and wake her up – everything is – I'm going to bring everything under control now just listen – YOU! New-girl-dash-union-girl! Put the phone down!

JUNE: What?

TRUMAN: Put the phone down.

JUNE: (*Into her headset.*) Excuse me one moment there is a problem with the line I need to put you on hold – (*To TRUMAN.*) I'm not falling for that.

TRUMAN: What?

JUNE: Don't answer the lines? So you'll have just cause to fire us? I'm not giving you just cause to fire us. You've got no earthly cause to fire us, and we derive strength from that fact. It's a management trick. I've seen it before.

TRUMAN: A management trick? I've never even heard of that.

ANDREW: I have. Yeah. I thought that's what you've been doing with Lucille.

TRUMAN: No.

ANDREW: What do you mean 'no'?

TRUMAN: I'm not running a management trick. No.

ANDREW: Then?

Pause.

Then why the hell are you letting them get away with it? With all this stuff? It's been what?

LUCILLE: Two years.

ANDREW: Two years or so – thank you Lucille – two years.

Pause.

Why have you been letting them get away with everything?

Long pause.

You let her drink!

Very long pause.

You're taking notes right? You're building a case? You're biding your time? You're thinking about? You have thought about it? You haven't even thought about it?

TRUMAN: I guess I just don't give a shit.

JUNE: Truman, join us in the walkout!

TRUMAN: I don't give a shit either way.

ANDREW: That's inspiring. Is that how you restore order
Truman? Everything is out of control and you don't care?
Fatherhood's loss, this guy, right Lucille? Had you been a
father you would have, no doubt, improved fatherhood for
generations to come. 'Truman' would be slang for 'father', if
only you had shared your wisdom with a son. To think that
some women are raised by slobs, fools, monsters, and here we
have Truman! Childless! Is this not an ancient Greek Tragedy?
Do we here not have, before us, a human Greek Tragedy? This
man. This Truman. A fucking saint. A fucking hero. A fucking
Man. Capital M.

Pause.

Don't make me laugh. Really don't even. Mark that it's mine.

TRUMAN: This is a test.

LUCILLE: (*Referring to the Strowger.*) Goddamn this thing.
(*LUCILLE spits.*) What is this thing Truman?

JUNE: He's management Lucille. And he isn't with us yet.

LUCILLE: What in God's name is it then? Truman just tell me,
I've turned a blind eye for too long.

TRUMAN: It's a Strowger.

Pause.

It's a –

LUCILLE: Explain its evolution to me.

TRUMAN: You mean who invented it?

LUCILLE: If you must.

ANDREW: I'll tell you its evolution: first there were fish, then
you, then this bright shiny baby over here.

TRUMAN: Arnold Strowger invented it.

LUCILLE: So you know the story?

TRUMAN: Sure I know the story.

LUCILLE: Pippa wake up, we're getting a story.

PHILIPPA: (*She wakes up.*) Tell me.

TRUMAN: It's not a story.

LUCILLE: Go ahead: 'Arnold Strowger invented it...'

TRUMAN: (*Pause.*) He was a funeral owner. And people in his area mostly –

LUCILLE: Which area?

TRUMAN: The middle west.

LUCILLE: Okay.

TRUMAN: Lots of dead people. Lots of competition. For funeral homes. And most people don't plan to use a home. They just call the operator. The operator decides. Out there. So he thought the girls were. Or might. You know. (*He points away from the Strowger.*) Directing traffic. For bribes. (*He mimes 'cash' between his fingers.*) And so: (*TRUMAN gestures to the automated switchboard.*)

PHILIPPA: What a charmer.

LUCILLE: So what he doesn't trust us this guy?

PHILIPPA: Whadda weasel this hump.

LUCILLE: What a ladies man this guy, someone hold me back.

PHILIPPA: Hold me back or I don't know what I'll do, I can barely contain myself.

LUCILLE: I'm practically in heat. I'm heating up. I'm burning up. I'm on fire. I'm having hot flashes. Oops it's menopause. Now I'm dead, he killed me. I'm dead now this guy is so incredible.

JUNE: Do you see how hostile it is? The sheer hostility of it.

LUCILLE: The guy has no, whadda call it, advertising strategy in his, you know, community, and we. suffer down the line. Whadda Prince. (*She spits on the ground.*)

JUNE: They've been planning this for years. The Union has managed to stabilize the situation somewhat, but we can't hold on without showing real numbers. Out there. In the streets.

ANDREW: Do you hear this? You're the reason we need this thing. You don't owe her any thank you. Stabilize the situation? Your lot's been around barely three years!

JUNE: And we've always been opposed to automation.

ANDREW: Yeah, always since three years ago. You're lots of help after the fact.

JUNE: The fact?

ANDREW: Of it! Existing!

JUNE: Darling, this thing wasn't a fact until Bell Atlantic adopted it seventy-two hours ago. Before that it was a hypothesis. It was a rumor. It was a fad.

ANDREW: Are you kidding? They've got these all over the place. I knew they'd come around upstairs. Good. I'm all for it. And temperance-prohibition for all the saps and slobs with houses too small to hide liquor in. It's called Progress.

JUNE: It's only progress if it's in my best interests. If it isn't in my best interests then it isn't progress. It's just something which screws things up for us. That's all it is.

LUCILLE: I've heard enough. I refuse this unholy thing entirely. Take it away.

PHILIPPA: Yes, take it away from here.

LUCILLE: Get it the hell outta here!

TRUMAN: Hold on. It's a trial. It's really just a trial is what they say. It's pointless, the whole thing, if no one likes it. And they don't know if people will like it. It's really just a trial.

LUCILLE: Like it? Liko? How could people like it. It isn't like them!

PHILIPPA: You're thinking 'doesn't like'. It doesn't like them.

LUCILLE: Isn't like, doesn't like, it's the same thing.

PHILIPPA: It isn't.

LUCILLE: It is in Latin, Pippa, I swear you flapper dumbbells are going to have some dumbbell children I swear to Christ.

PHILIPPA: Oh I'm sorry Latin.

TRUMAN: It's a trial. It's nothing if people don't like it.

ANDREW: Like it? What are we going to give them a choice? No choices. We're not giving choices.

TRUMAN: What do you know about it that I don't know.

ANDREW: Plenty.

TRUMAN: Yeah plenty.

ANDREW: I know plenty about it.

TRUMAN: Nothing I don't know.

ANDREW: Plenty you don't know. You don't know nothing.

TRUMAN: I've been here longer. I believe that counts for something.

ANDREW: Ever been to the company steam-room?

TRUMAN: The company steam-room?

ANDREW: Mm-hm.

Pause.

Tucking your kids into bed. The things you miss. Around here.

TRUMAN: Oh, well, not here, apparently. In the 'steam-room'. (*TRUMAN places finger quotations around 'steam-room'.*)

ANDREW: You might as well make little fingers around it 'cause it is a mirage as far as you know Sonny. You don't know how a company works.

TRUMAN: So what? So it's not a trial?

ANDREW: Not if I have anything to say about it.

PHILIPPA: Well do you?

Pause.

ANDREW: Maybe not. But in a few years.

LUCILLE: Well I challenge the goddamn thing to a race!

PHILIPPA: I challenge it to a dance competition. I've got some moves no robot could ever do.

LUCILLE: Thanks doll, pipe down.

PHILIPPA: Never ever do! (*PHILIPPA is behaving like LUCILLE, seated at her side.*) I challenge the Strowger to a tap-dancing contest to be judged by an assembled panel of top tap-dancing experts. And then we'll see who's the better dancer.

LUCILLE: She's drunk I think. To be sure. Ci scusiamo.

TRUMAN: It's a trial. It'll fail. People want to hear other people, that's the best thing we've got going, we don't want to improve on that. No one wants to buy a sandwich from a machine, why would they want to plug their own switches in their own homes.

ANDREW: They just dial a number Truman. It'll be a little longer.

TRUMAN: Or whatever they do.

ANDREW: They don't plug their own switches.

TRUMAN: It's impersonal. That's what it is.

JUNE: This is a bloody good-cop-bad-cop routine, we have it in England too you bloody fools you think I'm going to fall for that?

PHILIPPA: Which is the good cop?

JUNE: Listen to the two of you. Listen one says Bell Atlantic will crush us if we walkout, the other says 'stay inside, keep working, it's just a 'trial'. (*JUNE puts finger quotations around 'trial'.*)

ANDREW: Now you've got her doing it.

JUNE: It's a bloody good-cop-bad-cop! Don't you see it girls! They're running scared!

LUCILLE: All right hush your mouth we hear you.

PHILIPPA: It's a zany idea.

LUCILLE: These two? They're in love. They daren't, no darling. Understand me.

JUNE: We don't talk strategy around these men until they pledge.

LUCILLE: Pledge, pledge what?

JUNE: Pledge allegiance to our Cause! Our cause for solidarity. Workers! Us. (*She gestures at the women.*) Maybe them. (*She gestures at the men.*) Against the corporation. (*She gestures up, down, and all around.*) Get it?

LUCILLE: What? You want them to promise?

JUNE: It's a kind of promise. A much more severe promise yes. I want them to promise with the utmost severity.

LUCILLE: Okay so whatever they promise and maybe they lie anyway so let's move on. Moving on. Truman!

TRUMAN: What?

LUCILLE: Can we rig up a kind of race in here? Maybe a kind of thing between me and the Robot. A competition.

TRUMAN: The Strowger Automated Switching System?

LUCILLE: Fine. You're welcome.

TRUMAN: It isn't a wind-up Arab beating people at chess Lucille.

LUCILLE: Yeah sure, put a hat on it, whatever you need to do, and bring the brass downstairs huh? See me and Strowger, God rest, meet each other in exhibitionary combat? Sound like fun? Sure it does, set us up. Will ya? Go ahead.

TRUMAN: A combat for what? A competition to do what?

LUCILLE: For whose got the chops. Me or Strowger.

TRUMAN: At what Lucille? At what?

LUCILLE: Whadda ya think? At switching and all its particulars.

TRUMAN: Well it doesn't do the particulars.

LUCILLE: Which is just one of the reasons I ain't particularly scared of going head-to-head with the rookie over there.

TRUMAN: (*To ANDREW.*) We could do call volume. Call volume is really the only way to measure it.

ANDREW: Don't talk to me about it.

LUCILLE: Mano e mano. Whatever.

TRUMAN: So?

LUCILLE: Yeah, however you want to do it.

TRUMAN: I'll set it up for call volume.

PHILIPPA: Well I suppose if you're serious shouldn't I do it?

LUCILLE: You? No. You're my protégé.

PHILIPPA: What? I was swell before I worked with you.

LUCILLE: Truman! Let's get me over there.

TRUMAN grabs ANDREW and they begin to haul LUCILLE, chair and all, over in front of the stage-right switchboard currently occupied by JUNE. JUNE moves out of the way and takes her chair.

You don't work with me Pippa, let's face it, you work under me. And you're very good down there, you're learning, but this might be the fight of our lives, the last day, as it were, and a queen must lead her people in times of great tumultuousness and turmoil.

PHILIPPA: Yeah maybe turmoil I see your point.

JUNE: This is ridiculous. Pippa what's the matter with you? We need to stage a walkout! (*To LUCILLE.*) We have to stage a walkout.

PHILIPPA: A walkout, what's that?

JUNE: We just walk out.

PHILIPPA: Walk out where? Outside?

JUNE: For a start!

PHILIPPA: Then where do we go? Home?

JUNE: Not home. You stay outside the building.

PHILIPPA: And what? Throw eggs?

JUNE: No. You protest. You yell about what's happening.

PHILIPPA: But we're the only ones who care what's happening and only half of us do.

JUNE: You – I've been over this with the others – we just have to plead our case in public. Let our voices sing a song of injustice, scream until the foundations of this company are shaken to their very foundation.

PHILIPPA: What do they care? They've got our replacements lined up probably.

JUNE: That's why we need the cooperation of management.

ANDREW: No.

PHILIPPA: They'll just replace the management.

ANDREW: No.

JUNE: And so we hurl abuse at their new management, and shame them in the eyes of their fellow workers.

LUCILLE: His fellow worker is going to be too busy clamoring for his vacated position to perform the shaming upon which your protest is predicated. Nope. We're going to get the brass down here. Go ahead. Take a walk downstairs, get your fancy pantsy boys from the Union and go ahead and yell and shout about worker's rights and their inalienable indispensability to the Corporation. Meanwhile, I'm going to sit right there, and prove that promise true. On this very stage. As it were. Truman, let's get the brass down here, I'm making a spectacle of myself and all's not for nothing. I'm settling for nothing less than empirical evidence, God forgive me. Get the brass down here.

TRUMAN: Lu, I don't know any brass.

LUCILLE: Okay. You. Boy. What's your name?

ANDREW: Andrew??

LUCILLE: Get some brass down here boy.

ANDREW: You're crazy if you think I'm going to invite anyone from upstairs to this side-show.

LUCILLE: Alright damn it. We'll go ahead without the brass. I put my faith in the rumor mill by God. But let's also say that you are in charge of the rumor mill Pippa, capisci?

PHILIPPA: Chapash. Whatever. Yes. I'll tell everyone.

PHILIPPA is now seated on the floor next to LUCILLE. She looks like a pet.

ANDREW: You're wasting your goddamn time. You can't bat your lashes and make us give in to your demands.

LUCILLE: Empirical evidence! *Pardona mi Dio!*

ANDREW: (*To TRUMAN.*) And you, you sap. What are you? Demented now?

LUCILLE: Ready Truman?

TRUMAN: (*Bored.*) Yes.

JUNE: Can't you see it's a bloody good-cop-bad-cop?

ANDREW: Oh would you shut it? Believe me if I was trying to hatch a 'plan' or develop a 'routine' I wouldn't employ this worthless sack-of-shit. Right Sonny? This dribbling idiot. All these years.

TRUMAN: You call me Truman.

ANDREW: Hey, do me a favor, stop cheating death okay Truman? Quit ducking the Grim Reaper and die already you old bitch.

TRUMAN charges at ANDREW.

Don't you touch me you old ghost! Get the hell –

TRUMAN tackles ANDREW. They wrestle on the ground for a long time. Finally, TRUMAN punches ANDREW in the nose.

JUNE: Are you going to stand alone Miss? Is that it? Are you the pretty bird that never played ball? Is that your plan? You never gave in. You never gave up. You never stood beside a man. You never raised your voice in unison. You spoke alone. You slept alone. Your bed was rarely empty but you always slept alone, didn't you? You never stood for another man or woman did you? You never stood for a man or an idea that wasn't your own. You never begged. You never took your shoes off in public. Did you. You never apologized or compromised. You never sobered up. You never settled down. You never did. You left the world with no eulogy because you took all your friends with you. Didn't you. Didn't you? Won't you. Won't you leave a corpse with no scars weren't self-inflicted? Won't lend your name, your hand or your voice in solidarity with your own best interests! Not to mention your fellow man, your fellow woman. Solidarity With Your Fellow Man. You couldn't bare it. You wouldn't lend your hand, your name or your voice in solidarity with your fellow man? You died alone then? Is that how this all turns out for you? In your head? On your time? That's where it all arrives? And you can't change? Correct. Yes. I'm positive. Lovely. You stood alone Miss.

ANDREW: Ouch.

TRUMAN releases ANDREW and he stands up.

Is my nose bleeding?

TRUMAN: It isn't bleeding.

ANDREW: You've got some nerve.

JUNE: May I ask you briefly what kind of Christian refuses brotherhood? What kind of Christian worships at the feet of a corporation? What kind of Christian needs their own divinity reflected back to them from on high, knowing our hands belong in the soil: side-by-side with the hands of a man free and equal to us in every meaningful way? It is a cowardly Christian who can't speak to God directly, would rather send another man to do it for her. That's not a Christian. A Christian stands alone is not a Christian. A Christian who turns her back on brotherhood and sisterhood and sides with, hides with a corporation – and a church by the way I know you're a fucking Catholic by God you're bloody Italian – a woman who hides under the skirt of the Belle Atlantic instead of stepping in the street with her sisters is no proper Christian and no proper citizen as far as I'm concerned. I say to all here

assembled and offer no apology it's truth I speak about this
boozy wop thinks she's the queen of far as the eye can see.

*TRUMAN has returned to his position and holds his counter ready
to judge the race between LUCILLE and the Strowger. LUCILLE
drains her bottle of beer. There is no beat between the last swallow
of beer and the first sentence.*

LUCILLE: I'm a Catholic. That's true. And queen of far as
the eye can see. E vero. You're half-right kid. Hey English.
Ascolta! Don't I sound like royalty? I believe I speak directly
to God. And I ask him for things directly. We meet at four
a.m. every Monday, and I ask for things. Tom boys to lace my
corsets and braid my hair. Big-boned girls to blow me kisses. A
city of the future, large enough and regal enough to entertain
and delight me daily. A palace in the perfect shape of a cold-
water flat downtown. That's what I want. It's what I ask for
and what I get. A palace in disguise.

*LUCILLE opens a bottle of beer for TRUMAN. He takes it and
drinks.*

Vicious liquids to ease my boredom and lubricate my
interactions with the rest of you; to ignite my evening's
recreation and knock my mind into sleep. Vicious liquids to
cool and filter early morning sun. Vicious liquids to replace
naps. To prolong sex. To give me a good cry. I beg God
for one simple vicious liquid to cure all ailments and he
generously supplies me with many different and wonderful
varieties.

Pause.

And you say I'm not a good Christian? Then why am I so
beautiful? Why am I so goddamned beautiful? Because God
neglects me? No. Because he showers me with light. Perche lui
bagna con il' luce.

*Pause. She puts her headphones on her head and patches them into
her board.*

Pippa, Andiamo.

PHILIPPA: Hold on. I got the Micks on the line to cheer you on.

PHILIPPA plugs a switch and we hear the Irish operators from Boston again.

Okay, we're ready.

LUCILLE: Not these pigs. I hate these pigs.

Sounds of Irish women cheering.

Ms Kenny: Quiet down girls. Now I'm just calling to wish you luck Ms Lucille, and Godspeed in your endeavor.

LUCILLE: It's you Mick sows brought the Union down on me isn't it?

Ms Kenny: Not us, Ms Lucille. They sent you that Orange wench, June Cromwell, or whatever her name is, didn't they?

Boos and hissing from the Irish girls.

LUCILLE: She's preaching your message Kenny, she's in bed with you as far as I'm concerned.

Ms Kenny: Aw, but we don't like that one Lucille, she's a fuckin' pain in the arse.

Ms O'Murphy: Who, that big-eyed witch? Oh, I can't stand her. From Philadelphia?

LUCILLE: I'm about to spear the dragon in the name of Roman Popery you billy-goat heathens, mind my steam.

Ms Kenny: Have at it, ya wee peasant dyke.

LUCILLE: Let the exhibitionary competition, begin!

TRUMAN: Alright we're starting.

TRUMAN moves to flip a switch on the back of the Strowger. Suddenly we hear a loud mechanical snap followed by what sounds like a microphone pop. TRUMAN jerks his hand away, terrified.

LUCILLE: Jesus! (*LUCILLE jerks her headset off in pain.*) Jesus what
was that?

*There is a sudden rush of noise from the Strowger and from
LUCILLE's board.*

TRUMAN: That's it. We've started.

LUCILLE: Jesus. Start counting.

*LUCILLE swings around to face her board while pulling her
headphones back on. We hear her voice buried in noise of the lines.*

*The following soundscape should interweave dialing noises with
old-fashioned voices reciting numbers and saying surnames, along
with two distinct noises signifying connecting calls from both boards.
After a few moments the Strowger should take an obvious lead.*

Number please? – thanks pal – we're not repeating it back
anymore, new policy – Polly? Mom or sister? – Got it
love ya doll – number please? – four-nine-twelve? – got it
– Connecticut? Connecticut twelve over to you – number
please? – got it – number please? – got it – thanks Mac you
sound husky – yeah I said it – number please? – Paul? How's
yer kid? Nah. 'Cause you didn't baptize him that's why – get
outta here – eighty-eight? Got it – number please? – Say
China? Hold on – Is Strowger taking internationals I don't
think so – I'm sending this over through Alaska – Anchorage?
Anchorage? Hey you blubber-lover take this line to China
– number please? Got it – Yeah? – Oh yeah someone
important I bet – who is it? – who is it or I won't connect you
– the President you say? I'd be proud to connect him – I didn't
vote for him but I respect him just the same – you tell 'em
– number please?

TRUMAN: Not doing so good here Lucille.

PHILIPPA: Come on Lu I'm your protégé!

LUCILLE: I'm giving it everything I got – And to you sir
– You're welcome – number please? Chittenden County

– Lafayette Place – Branding Iron Lane – number please?
– Denmark Sweden? – Denmark, Maine – got it – number
please – Bob and Sandy – for the Linda Allens got it – number
please – K for James number please – oh it's the big house
huh? What's this boy, lawyer or mother? Good boy. Say strong
– number please –

*LUCILLE stretches her right arm out and begs a drink from
PHILIPPA.*

– Nurse, someone put some lemonade in my lemonade I'm
dry – number please? – Sure thing – number please? – Just
fine and how are you? – Glad to hear it – I'm not sweatin' it
– number please? – You Italian? Where are you? New Jersey?
Come la tua famiglia abittano in New Jersey?

*PHILIPPA hands LUCILLE a big drink. She holds it
outstretched.*

You know why New York Italians are so depressed? 'Cause the
light at the end of the tunnel is New Jersey – number please –

*LUCILLE tosses her full drink on the Strowger. There is a spark.
The whole cacophony comes to a grinding halt.*

ANDREW: What the hell do you think you're doing?

LUCILLE: So I'm disqualified! It doesn't count as a loss! (*She
crosses herself. Then, to God:*) Pardon mi Dio.

ANDREW: That's it. I'm shutting this whole disgraceful mess
down. No more power for you. Stay, go, I don't care, we'll
starve you out if we have to. I'll build a chimney around you.
Endgame. Night night. I'm exiting. Screw off.

ANDREW exits.

JUNE: You're crooked.

LUCILLE: So you don't like New York City?

JUNE: You're crooked forever. You're crooked inside.

LUCILLE: What's the right thing anyway? What is that thing?

JUNE: Rotten like this rotten hot garbage city.

LUCILLE: That's because you don't see a street the way I see
a street. You don't understand the relationship between the
buildings and the sky. You don't see where the ground is.
I see all the stains. The long gone ones even. The good with
the bad.
I see rivers in the gutters of gin and tears.
I hear tongues, of all sizes. Pink ones and red ones and long
ones. I hear every part from tip to root. It's basically English.
You don't see a street the way I see a street. When I'm
cruising.
When strangers make eyes at each other I can smell their
children.
I can see underneath your fingernails and in the corners of
your eyes.
You know – the inside corners where your brain throws away
all the ugly thoughts for you to pick and flick in the morning.
Where God puts tears. That corner. Where I'm at.

There is a sudden blackout. ANDREW has pulled the plug.

And anyway streets aren't streets to me, they're stages. And it's
clear to me as if I wrote it.
This island is Rome. This city is my church. This office is that
booth. Where flesh is disciplined on the line. Where my voice
may act as my soul promises to be: unrestricted and eternal.
And I am a soldier. Six days a week we will conquer the
World. On the seventh, let us conquer ourselves.

JUNE: You mistook the dollar bill for a papal indulgence. A
treasurer's signature won't put you in heaven.

PHILIPPA: Would you get out of here already? Jesus.

JUNE: Truman?

TRUMAN: Nah.

JUNE exits. PHILIPPA pours LUCILLE a fresh drink.

LUCILLE: Dear God keep me from the hysterical masses which
    pepper the mid-drift of this otherwise healthy American
    body. Forgive them. They are Protestants. Nearly all of them.
    A tin ear for drama and green thumb for digging up dirt.
    God forgive them their awful, boring diaries and near sexual
    longing for the task of chopping wood. I know you hate a
    man on his knees praying in the dirt. I know you hate an
    unforgiving Prod. But you love a Catholic with the bottom of
    her glass raised in prayer. You love a party God. You love to
    party God.

PHILIPPA: 'Party' ain't a verb.

LUCILLE: It is now, and from now on shall be, Amen.

PHILIPPA: She could've been your sister.

LUCILLE: I don't have any sisters.

PHILIPPA: I met your sister.

LUCILLE: That isn't a sister, that's what I left behind in my
    mother.

PHILIPPA: Your sister is married with two children.

LUCILLE: My point exactly.

PHILIPPA: She's probably a foot taller than you.

LUCILLE: Who said height was part of human progress?

PHILIPPA: Darwin probably.

LUCILLE: What's in a name?

TRUMAN: (*Reading his framed clipping, beer in hand.*) Always a
    message for someone, bringing them smiles and tears.
    Joy or sorrow, or weal or woe, and so we drift with the years.
    Listening always and ever, never missing a call,
    The love of the Gracious Master above and over us all.

The reaper calls for our number. A mound on a sun-kissed hill,
There's a line gone down or in trouble, and the voice of the
world is still.

LUCILLE: Sentimental.

PHILIPPA: I don't think you understand silence Lucille.

LUCILLE: What? What's to understand? (*Pause.*) What? Che
silenzia? It's nothing. It means niente. (*Longer pause.*) What
are you being silent now? Very clever. Why don't you explain
the difference between silence and boredom. (*Silence.*) Okay.
Fine. You're just proving my point. Silence is just the absence
of words. It's waiting. It's boredom. I'll prove it. Va bene.
(*Silence.*) And it's impossible. On top of being boring.

LUCILLE's board rings.

PHILIPPA: Are we mourning something?

TRUMAN: No.

LUCILLE's board rings again.

PHILIPPA: Well.

LUCILLE answers her line.

LUCILLE: Number please?

*The line is dead. We hear a modern day telephone disconnection
sound. It hums.*

Curtain.